What Every Contractor Should Know

What Every Contractor Should Know

✦

Answers to Real World Licensing Questions for California, Nevada and Arizona

David Kalb, President
Capitol Services Inc.

iUniverse, Inc.
New York Lincoln Shanghai

What Every Contractor Should Know
Answers to Real World Licensing Questions for California, Nevada and Arizona

This book may be ordered by contacting www.cutredtape.com

iUniverse
2021 Pine Lake Road, Suite 100
Lincoln, NE 68512
www.iuniverse.com
1-800-Authors (1-800-288-4677)

ISBN: 0-595-34551-4

Printed in the United States of America

Disclaimer

The questions, answers and general information in this book have been prepared by David Kalb for informational purposes only and are not to be considered legal advice. This book is provided as an informational guide to contractors licensing in California and other States. While the answers contained herein have been carefully researched, the reader is cautioned that recent changes to state laws or regulations can impact licensing requirements. Please note that the contractors licensing questions are situational. Therefore, responses to questions may not affect you the same way.

It is recommended that you confirm all licensing requirements prior to contracting, signing any contract, or making changes to your existing license. You may contact the author, David Kalb, through his web site, cutredtape.com. He would then have the opportunity to research and discuss your specific licensing issues.

You may also want to contact the Contractors State Licensing Board. Unless otherwise noted, the information herein is only relevant and applicable to California or the designated State mentioned in a specific question or answer.

This book is dedicated to the memory of my father, Marcus and my Uncle Abe Levine. Both had the confidence to support the idea of this 20-something starting Capitol Services in 1982 and encouraging me every step of the way.

Contents

ACKNOWLEDGEMENTS

FIRST AND FOREMOST, I WOULD LIKE TO THANK THE THOUSANDS of readers of my column who, for the past decade, have provided the questions contained in this book. This book would not have been possible without the calls, emails and fax questions that I receive on a daily basis from contractors throughout California and across the United States.

I appreciate the numerous Builders Exchanges and Associations up and down the state that provide their membership with this resource and the publications, including *California Builder and Engineer* and *Daily Pacific Builder* that publish my column on a regular basis.

Thank you to Everett Lawson, a former CSLB licensing deputy, who was kind enough to review these responses prior to publication.

I appreciate former California Registrar of Contractors John Maloney's kind words in the Forward of this book.

Finally, I am very grateful to Rick Reed, who has read every one of my 400+ columns. His contribution and editing each week has helped me present a better experience for the reader.

PREFACE

It has always been my goal to "Simplify State Government" for contractors and construction-industry businesses that must deal with State government agencies.

While mediating problems for California's Governor, I specialized in helping contractors who were having problems with State government. After four years in the Governor's Office, I started Capitol Services, a business/government-consulting firm based in Sacramento.

In 1995, I began writing a weekly Q & A column for contractors. The column is published statewide in over 30 industry publications. *What Every Contractor Should Know* is a compilation of the most relevant and current questions from people like you.

Once referred to as the "Rambo of Red Tape" by *California Republic* magazine, The Los Angeles Times ran a feature on Capitol Services, Inc. in their Business Section titled *Making a Living From Cutting Red Tape*. It was a natural to select **cutredtape.com** as my Internet address.

An excerpt from an article in *Construction Data Magazine* may best sum up my background. "He has never designed, developed, or manufactured a product. He is not a construction man, yet the Pacific Coast Builder's Conference recognized him as an expert. Thousands of contractors across the country—many of them with little time to waste—have called Capitol Services to help them in California".

FOREWORD

September 14, 2004

Every once in a while a book comes along that fits a need. This book provides specific, practical and accurate informative answers to questions that impact almost every person, partnership or corporation that requires a contractor's license.

Like most laws in the Business and Professions Code, the Contractor's License Law attempts to codify the process of acquiring and maintaining a contractor's license. This is obviously complicated by the organizational structure of the licensee (i.e. corporation, sole proprietorship, responsible managing employee, etc.) as well as what type of license or licenses are required (electrical, plumbing, underground to high rises). Add to this the administrative interpretations of the Contractors Board as well as the Courts, and you've started a beautiful dance through the bureaucracy of State government. Your dance card can also add partners that inter-relate to the contractors law—from the Department of Industrial Relations, Employment Development and Cal Trans, to the Secretary of State, and FTB. Just what a hard working contractor wants to hear to what was deemed a perfectly simple question.

I've had the pleasure of working with the author when he was employed by the California Governor's office and as a private consultant. During those years he's helped a great many people and developed the practical information in this book. I highly recommend that it be read by any of us in the Construction industry.

Your initial reaction might be to consider it boring, having no immediate application, or just something to help you sleep. Mark this writer's words; there's a question and answer in these chapters that'll wake you up and the sweat will start.

In closing, based on my experience, these comments apply as much to the corporate attorney as to a small contractor.

Good reading!

John Maloney,
California Registrar of Contractors, 1980-1988

1

Getting and Growing your Contractor's License

Getting your License Introduction

The most asked questions relate to securing a new contractors license. How do you apply? What are the minimum qualifications? How many years experience must I show? Is testing required? What about the bond amount? What do I need to do if I'm licensed in another State? What classification do I apply for? Do I need a license to handle 'handyman' work? Did someone mention Fingerprints? Read on for the answer to these and other practical questions on getting that contractors license.

Expanding Your License Introduction

Most contractors start with one license and one classification. Many stay with their first license and continue with the same name and number for years. For some contractors, their situation may change or new opportunities may present themselves. It may be necessary through expansion or changing the way you conduct business to apply for a new license or additional trade.

For instance changing your business name with the CSLB may seem like a simple procedure. However, if this change is going from a sole owner to a corporate license, a completely new application will be required. In some instances, a new number may be necessary.

With the change in the general building classification several years ago, some contractors have decided to apply for additional classifications to insure they're complying with all Board regulations. A "B" can handle any number of trades on a given project but cannot do just one trade such as plumbing, electrical or drywall—unless they hold that specific specialty class or sub to the proper specialty subcontractor.

In some instances securing an added class can be done with no testing.

Q: I received a call from the CSLB notifying me that my license application has been posted and that someone will be calling in about a month to set up a test date. He said that test date would likely be three to four weeks from when they call. The caller also said that we could expect to have a license in hand soon.

A: That call you received was NOT from the Contractors Board. I researched the status of your application and it's not close to being reviewed. The CSLB does NOT call applicants to tell them they have an upcoming test! The Board will notify you by mail regarding the time and place of your exam.

When you apply for a contractor's license your business name and address are put on the CSLB computer system. This becomes public information and is available for anyone who might like to contact you. There are a few companies that gather this information and call applicants inferring they work for the CSLB. Unfortunately the caller often gives out misinformation. They are simply trying to sell you something. If the "Contractors Board" contacts you in the future, ask the caller point blank if they work for the State of California. If they do not, tell them you're not interested in what they're selling.

Q: I was scheduled to take the contractor's license exam but did not show up at the scheduled time. The testing center said I would need to reschedule. When I received my notice from the Contractor's Board, it said I would need to reapply all over again. Can you tell me why?

A: This is not going to be good news. The CSLB allows most applicants who fail to appear for an exam to take it again by paying a $50.00 rescheduling fee. However, in your case, this was the SECOND time you failed to show for the exam, so the Board cancelled your application. Unfortunately, you will now need to file a new license application.

If an applicant does not think he or she will be able to make their scheduled exam date, it is highly advisable to notify the CSLB as soon as possible. By asking to have your test rescheduled, the Board will not count this against you. Applicants who fail to appear and do not have a valid reason (such as a medical emergency), will go to the bottom of the stack for rescheduling. This may mean a wait of months for your next test date.

Applicants you take the test and receive a failing score, can retake it, unlimited times, within an 18-month period with no penalty (they too must pay the $50.00 fee).

Q: I think I read in your column about the Board fingerprinting contractors. Is this still going to happen? I have been a contractor for 22 years and wonder if I'll have to go through this. What can you tell me about this issue?

A: CSLB fingerprinting authority was granted by the Legislature in 2002. Business and Professions Code Section 7069(b) states, "As part of an application for a contractor's license, the board shall require an applicant to furnish a full set of fingerprints for purposes of conducting a criminal record check".

As a long time contractor you will not need to be fingerprinted unless you apply for a new contractor's license. In implementing this program it was determined that all individuals on licenses in existence as of January 1, 2005 — or applications received prior to that date — will be exempt from fingerprinting. However, if someone such as yourself—who is exempt—applies for a new license, additional class, or to replace the qualifier on an existing license after January 1,2005 they would become subject to fingerprinting.

The definition of an applicant includes each officer, director, partner, associate, responsible managing employee (RME) or home improvement salesperson.

The CSLB is charged with determining whether an applicant has committed acts or crimes, which are grounds for denial of licensure. They have the authority to consider a broad range of criminal convictions and fingerprinting is one tool they will use to determine if licensure should be granted. There is no hard and fast list to report which crimes will prevent licensure and which will be allowed.

Q: I want to add my son to my license. How can I do this? Will he need to take an exam?

A: As indicated in our discussion, since you have a sole owner license, your son could only be added if he qualifies a classification OTHER THAN the one you hold. The CSLB will not allow two people to simultaneously qualify the same class on the same license.

Since your son is not presently qualified to hold a California contractor's license, your options are to form a corporation or partnership. By listing your son as an officer or partner you will give him the opportunity to gain the 4 years experience to qualify for his own license. Four years of journeyman level work in the trade(s) is a minimum requirement. Whether he will need to sit for an exam depends on what laws and regulations are in effect at the time he files an application.

Q: I'm interested in doing 'handyman' work. Some jobs may bill out higher than $500 and may include installing lights, cabinets and drywall—no real construction (structural that is). I understand that one must spend 4 years as a journeyman before applying for a license. Is there a faster way? Is there more than one type of license? Can you suggest some help?

A: In order to secure a contractor's license you must be able to document at least 4 years (full-time) experience in the trade you're applying for. This must be at a journeyman level or above. You may be able to receive credit for up to two years experience if you have a 4-year college degree. There is no "faster" way to qualify for the license. The trades you list fall into 3 different classifications, the "C-10", "C-6" and "C-9". I suggest you apply for the trade where you have the most experience.

Q: It's my understanding that a bond for $10,000 is required so a contractor's license can become 'active'. My question is, instead of a bond can cash be substituted?

A: YES, you have the option of posting $10,000 cash or Certificate of Deposit (CD) in lieu of the contractors bond. Once this CD or cash is filed with the CSLB, they can hold it up to 4 years after your license expires. This allows for a "discovery" period in case there is a problem with your work that is not immediately identified. The bond amount is scheduled to increase to $12,500 on January 1, 2007.

Q: If you have had a felony conviction, can you still become a licensed contractor in the State of California? What if the felony was not a violent crime?

A: Being convicted of a felony does not exclude you from securing a contractor's license. It depends on the nature of the crime, whether the person is on parole or probation and if the crime was "construction related". The CSLB will also weigh whether the applicant has repeatedly been convicted of criminal activities.

For the purpose of denying a license, the Board will consider if the crime was substantially related to the functions or duties of a contractor licensee. These crimes may include, but are not limited to, submitting false vouchers to obtain construction loan funds; not using funds for stated construction purposes; theft of building materials or equipment from a construction project; embezzlement; and violation of various contractor licensing laws.

Q: I worked for my father as a journeyman plumber for 14 years (he is licensed in CA). I am considering taking over his business because he will retire soon. I need additional info about licensing etc…. Is there a way for me to take over his business and his license or do I need to get licensed first? Any information you can share would be appreciated.

A: Based on the information provided, you should be able to take over the family business after your father retires. By showing that you have been actively engaged in your father's plumbing business — for at least five of the past seven years — the Contractors Board will consider issuing you a license with a "family" waiver of the law and trade tests. An application must be filed for a new C-36 license and you must document that you're qualified in this trade and have been officially employed in the "family business". You may also request that your father's license number be reassigned to you. To secure this waiver, your father must state in writing that he no longer intends on conducting business as a contractor.

Q: We are a product manufacturer based in the Midwest. Our product is sold to distributors in California and Arizona for sale to the end user (such as schools). We are now being told that our distributors need to be licensed as contractors. I read one of your recent columns (on the internet) and would like your opinion on this issue.

A: (Section 7026 of the B&P Code) is the basis for answering your question. As we discussed, your agreement with these distributors is to provide a product that they install for the end user. Although the work is being performed by a licensed contractor, in effect this is being 'sub-contracted' by the distributor. 7026 (Contractor" Defined) states in part, "a contractor is any person who undertakes…or purports to have the capacity to undertake…or does…through others, construct, alter, repair, add to...". Your distributor, because of their arrangement with the contractor, would fall within this definition.

Q: I recently passed my license exam and was given a yellow book "ASBESTOS: A Contractor's Guide and Open Book Examination". I don't handle any asbestos and never will, so why does this need to be completed?

A: This "Open Book Asbestos Exam" is required of all applicants but does not authorize you or your company to remove asbestos. This is intended to make you aware of the risks posed by asbestos and to give you a knowledge base in case you inadvertently encounter asbestos during any project you may work on. Among the goals of this booklet are to: make you familiar with what materials are suspected to contain asbestos; reporting requirements; who can legally remove asbestos; and methods for avoiding contact with asbestos containing materials.

Q: Is it legal to do any work over $500.00 after you have filled an application for a license? I have passed the Law exam and have incorporated my business. Can I now bid and perform work before passing the trade and obtaining my license? Please advise.

A: Unfortunately, you cannot legally do any work in CA (over $500) until you have a contractor's license number. The license must be in the same name as on your contract and must remain in good standing throughout the entire time you are working. Technically you should not even be bidding work until you're licensed. If you're going to do this work under the corporation, I would suggest filing another original license application with a note that you have already passed the law portion. If you wait until the individual license is issued and then apply for the corporate license it will take much longer to receive the proper license number.

Q: Is there anything in the CSLB codes that expressly prohibits a company from paying a contractor to use their contractor's license number?

A: There are two sections of the Business and Professions (B&P) Code that apply if someone is "paying to use someone else's license".

Section 7114 of the B&P code states that "aiding and abetting an unlicensed person to evade the provisions of this (licensing) chapter or conspiring with an unlicensed person or allowing one's license to be used by an unlicensed person…constitutes a cause for disciplinary action. This means the person 'lending' his license number will likely be issued a citation and could ultimately have his license suspended or revoked by the CSLB.

On the other hand, the unlicensed contractor who is "buying" the use of this license is subject to a hefty fine and could end up going to county jail. Section 7028 (B&P Code) states that it is a misdemeanor for any person to engage in the business or act in the capacity of a contractor without having a contractors license. Using someone else's license number does not constitute "having a contractors license"

In my twenty plus years of working with contractors, I have certainly seen and heard of this type of arrangement. Frankly, I do not understand why a contractor would consider this arrangement and jeopardize his existing license!

As for the unlicensed company, they face the prospect of not being paid for work performed. If a contract dispute is taken to court, and it was shown that the "contractor" was unlicensed, he would not be able to collect any monies due. All it takes is one unhappy customer or one surprise visit by the CSLB enforcement unit and this entire arrangement goes in the toilet.

Q: Does an architect need a contractor's license? Can an architect qualify to take the contractor's exam?

A: To your first question, the answer is NO. Section 7051 of the B&P Code states that no contractor's license is required if acting solely in your professional capacity as a licensed architect. To your second question, I can only respond with a definitive "maybe". Everyone's background is different.

To qualify as a contractor and sit for the contractor's license exam, you must show 4 years (full time) experience within the past 10 years in the trade you'll be applying for. This work should be field related (journeyman, foreman, project management) and not "administrative" in nature (i.e. contracts, purchasing, etc.). If you oversee construction projects, you should be able to show that this experience is beyond your capacity as a licensed architect.

Q: I only have two years experience in the building trades but I have a degree in Construction Management. Can I qualify for a contractor's license?

A: The Contractors Board will accept education in lieu of experience qualifications. Depending on the college degree you hold and the classification you're applying for, the CSLB will give you up to three years credit. In your case, a degree in Construction Management combined with two full years working in the building trades (framing, concrete, roofing, etc.) should allow you to take the "B" test. If, for instance, you were applying for the "A" (general engineering) classification, and held an engineering degree, the Board would likely credit you three of the required four years experience.

Q: Why should I get my contractor's license? I've been working for nearly 10 years and have never had any problems. I simply avoid projects where I need to pull a permit. Even if I get caught, what can the state do?

A: You like to live dangerously! The Contractors State License Board regularly conducts sting operations throughout the state. They also monitor advertising in local publications and look for ads that do not have a license number. You may have avoided being caught for 10 years but that next quote may be your undoing. There are several laws on the books that allow the CSLB to fine you—up to $15,000—for working without a license.

Since you're a subcontractor, it is illegal for any licensed general contractor to hire you. Doing so could put their license in jeopardy. This certainly has a limiting effect on the number of jobs you may obtain.

Since you can only legally work on projects up to $500, it does not make much sense to avoid licensing. Your total cost including the state fee, bond, study materials and professional assistance with the application would likely not exceed $1,300. You do not even need workers compensation unless you hire employees. Get a license. One extra project per year would more than pay for this investment.

Q: I am about to be issued my contractor's license. Am I required to have my license number on my vehicle? Also, I know my phone book ad and contracts must have my number but what about other types of advertising?

A: It 's safe to say that all forms of advertising should carry your contractor's license number. Specifically this would include newspaper advertising, business cards, signs identifying you as a contractor, brochures, etc. Business and Professions (B&P) Code section 7030.5 says in part that contractors are required to include their license number in all construction contracts…and all forms of advertising as prescribed by the Registrar of Contractors". Board rule 861 clarifies this Code section.

If you're advertising on your truck it should carry your license number. However, if you are a plumbing, electrical sign or well-drilling contractor, all business vehicles MUST display your permanent business address and license number on both sides. You may wish to contact the CSLB for a free brochure titled *Advertising Do's and Don'ts for Contractors.*

Q: I have an expired "C-39" contractor's license. My dad has an inactive "B" license. We want to combine them in some way. Can I be his RME? Do we have any other options?

A: Yes, yes, yes. One option would be to reactivate your father's license and add you as an RME. This is allowed since you qualify a different classification. A second option would be to apply for a new license (such as a partnership) thereby combining both classifications. You might also consider applying for a Joint Venture license (that should only take a week to secure). If you elect to go with this third option, you would need to renew your license and your dad would be required to reactivate his. Joint Venture licenses are only allowed if all entities are licensed, active and in good standing.

Q: I would like to have my son qualify for his own license without taking any test. I was told that he could get his own license because he has been a company officer for 13 years and has been working in this trade since he was 18. Can we make this happen?

A: It does not appear that your son is eligible for a waiver of the license exam. According to my research, your son has never been listed as an officer on your corporate license. He may, in fact, be a Vice President but was never added to the CSLB's official records. Up until September 2003, an officer could have applied for his own license with a waiver; however, the Registrar virtually eliminated granting this type of waiver (7065.1 a)

Q: I want to change our business name with the CSLB. Is there a simple form?

A: Yes, the Contractors Board has a one page "Application for Changing Business Name". However, since you're licensed as a corporation, you must first change the name with the Secretary of State's Office. This requires filing an amendment to your articles of incorporation and providing proof of this amendment to the CSLB. Researching name availability is strongly suggested.

If you do not want to go through the added step with the Secretary of State, simply add a 'DBA' to your existing license using the above referenced form.

Q: I recently heard something about a "back-up license". What is a back-up license?

A: There is no official "back-up" contractor's license. Generally this term refers to an individual who holds a second (usually sole owner) contractor's license while the corporation or partnership holds the primary license with another qualifying individual. In this way, should something happen to the primary qualifier (RME or RMO) this "back-up" can be plugged in at short notice with no testing required. Some companies want a second officer or employee to have a license to make any sudden, unexpected transitions go smoothly.

Q: I read in one of your columns that an individual may only qualify 3 contractor licenses at a time. Are there any exceptions to this?

A: There are two general exceptions to B&P Code Section 7068.1(d) which states that "a qualifying individual may act as qualifier for no more than three firms in any one-year period." Since this section relates to partnerships and corporations, an individual may still hold a sole-owner (i.e. fourth) license.

The second exception allows a single corporation to simultaneously 'Do Business As' (DBA) several additional companies using the same Responsible Managing Individual (RME/RMO). For example, it could work as follows. A licensed contractor — we'll call XYZ Roofing Inc.—purchases 4 roofing companies throughout California. XYZ wants to continue using these well-established business names but wants all work conducted under the parent company. They may legally apply for 4 new contractor licenses all of which would be "XYZ Roofing,

Inc dba…" Once completed, the CSLB will have allowed 5 contractor licenses with one qualifier because this is still considered "one firm".

Q: I heard you could get an additional license with no testing. Is this true? What is the process and can I get a "C-57" (Well Drilling) classification without an exam?

A: The CSLB has always allowed licensed contractors to apply for an additional classification; however, since 1990, applicants have been able to request a waiver of the trade exam. Section 7065.3 states that "an examination may be waived for an additional classification under very strict and limited situations". At a minimum, the qualifier must have been listed on a license (active and in good standing) for 5 of the last 7 years and have had 4 years experience (within the past 10 years) in the trade being applied for. The Registrar of Contractors in 1990 adopted additional strict guidelines to implement this law. Subsequent Registrars can — and have — changed these guidelines.

For specialty "C" classifications (such as HVAC, Plumbing, Electrical, Sheet Metal, Concrete, etc.) the class being applied for must be "closely related to the class held". For instance, the Board has determined that boiler (C-4) and plumbing (C-36) are related, just as the C-35 (plastering) and C-9 (drywall) are similar enough to be considered for a waiver.

For general contractors (A or B) "the requested specialty class must be a significant component of the applicants general business". Although not specifically addressed in the regulations, an existing "A" (general engineering" contractor may be able to secure a "B" (general building) classification with a waiver (and visa versa). More likely are the connections between the "B" and common building trades such as concrete, plumbing, drywall, painting, roofing, and carpentry or the "A" and pipeline, demolition or structural steel.

Regarding the C-57, this is one of a half dozen classifications the CSLB has determined are not generally related to any other classification and therefore, not likely to be granted a waiver.

Q: I would like some information regarding hazardous waste licensing. What is required and how do I apply?

A: The State of CA requires contractors who engage in Hazardous Substance Removal to obtain a "Hazardous Waste" certification. Only those contractors holding the "A" (general engineering); "B" (general building); "C-12 (earthwork and paving); "C-36" (plumbing); "C-61/D-40" (service station maintenance) or "C-57" (water well drilling) classification may apply. The CSLB requires all applicants to file a one-page application and pass a 2 1/2 hour exam that is given daily throughout the state.

2

A's, B's and Specialty Licenses

One from Column "A" Introduction

Jack be nimble, Jack be quick, Jack jump over the candlestick. This old nursery rhyme could be used to categorize the construction industry and general engineering contractors in particular. The need to be agile; the ability to change directions swiftly; and the foresight to jump before you get burned.

In today's highly competitive contracting environment, nimble is—or should be — the operative word. I regularly field questions from "A" contractors regarding whether they're legally able to handle various types of projects. For instance, a caller asked if an "A" contractor could properly perform underground utility work—including electrical conduits. A city building department told him his company must also hold the "C-10" (electrical) classification.

The "A" is an extremely broad classification in that it encompasses a wide variety of subject areas. It includes irrigation and drainage; harbors and docks; dams and levees; bridges and underpasses; water and sewer; and parks and playgrounds to name just a few. General engineering contractors regularly bid as a prime with the option of subcontracting major portions. An "A" can also bid as a subcontractor. The "A" encompasses most (if not all) work that can be handled by the following specialty classifications: C-12 (earthwork and paving), C-34 (pipeline) and C-42 (sanitation systems). In many instances an "A" can handle Parking and Highway Improvements (C-32); erect structural steel (C-51) and yes, even build swimming pools (C-53).

With all this being said, a general engineering contractor CANNOT do it all. There are limitations. A caller was surprised to learn that as an "A" he could not bid on renovating public school buildings or for that matter build the school. This would fall under a "B" (general building) contractor. The "A" is not at the top of the construction 'food chain'.

One from Column "B" Introduction

The "B" is the most sought after classification by far. More people hold the general building class than any other. There are over 140,000 "B" contractors in CA. The next closest are the "C-10" and "A" with 29,000 and 20,000 licensees respectively.

As common as the "B" is, it is also one of the most misunderstood classifications licensed by the CSLB. Over the 75 years that contractors have been regulated, this classification has undergone changes. Most recently, the "Home Depot decision" redefined what a "B" could and could not do.

Some contractors believe the "B" is all encompassing and that any trade can be performed under this class. NOT SO. For instance fire sprinkler work cannot be performed without holding (or subcontracting to) a "C-16". Sure, a "B" can perform general construction projects that contain numerous trades; however, they CANNOT perform the same work if only one trade is involved. Contract for a room addition or remodel or build a new house with a "B", but do not, for instance, enter into an agreement for the plumbing, electrical, or painting ONLY—unless you hold that specialty class or use an appropriately licensed subcontractor. The two exceptions: Rough Framing "C-5"/Finish Carpentry "C-6". The "B" allows this work to be performed (although it is only one trade).

Herein lies the paradox in the "B" classification. When can you legally handle a project with one, two, or several trades? The questions in this chapter may hold the answer.

Q: I would like you to email me information regarding obtaining my General contractor license. I would like to start my own LLC eventually and need to know what classification is required to do so. Could you please explain to me the difference between a Class "A" and a Class "B" license.

A: First, forget about forming a LLC if you want to secure a contractor's license. The Contractors Board will not issue a license to a Limited Liability Company (LLC). Your second point about what "classification is required (to secure a contractors license)" is a bit backwards. Rather, you secure the license classification based on your trade experience. For instance, let's look at the "A" and "B"

The "A" class is general engineering. This requires the applicant to have at least 4 years practical experience in at least one, if not several, of the following areas: roads, streets, water supply, flood control, bridges, railroads, sewers, waste reduction plants, recreational works, power plants, underground utilities, shipyards, ports, pipelines, etc. The "B" (general building) classification requires 4 years experience in framing and at least two other unrelated trades such as plumbing, electrical, roofing, concrete, etc. There are 42 different classifications ranging from acoustics (C-2) and boiler (C-4) to well drilling (C-57) and welding (C-60). There are also thirty additional "limited specialties".

Q: We have an "A" and "B" license. Can we bid and self-perform the mechanical portion of an industrial or public works project if we do not have the required specialty licenses?

A: Yes! With an "A" and "B" license a contractor can legally handle most any portion of an industrial facility such as a refinery, chemical plant or powerhouse. On public projects such as a water treatment plant, sewage disposal facility or recreational work, the same would be true. This would include the boiler, electrical, process piping and other mechanical trades. Please realize there are always exceptions so it's important to evaluate each project individually to determine if this applies.

Q. Both my partner and I want to acquire an "A" and "B" contractor's license. Can we qualify the same license?

A: First you will need to decide what type of license you wish to apply for. Do you want to form a 'partnership'? Are each of you interested in obtaining individual licenses? Have you considered forming a corporation?

Since the CSLB will only allow you to apply for one classification at a time, you each should decide weather the 'A' or 'B' is a priority. I might suggest that one of you apply for the General Engineering (A) and the other initially go for the General Building (B). Then once you have qualified for the first classification, you can apply to add the other. You cannot qualify the same class on the same license.

Q: I've read many of your past columns and have often seen where a question arises regarding the proper classification on a project. After reviewing the list of Contractor classifications, I'm confused. Can I use my 'A' to do landscaping?

A: Both the General Engineering (A) and Landscaping (C-27) classifications are very broad. Each can encompass a number of trades such as concrete, plumbing, and electrical depending on the scope and location of the project. As we discussed, in your case, the job is a custom residential development. Therefore, in my opinion, it would NOT be appropriate to handle the irrigation, sod and patios under the 'A'. I would recommend applying for an additional C-27 classification.

On the other hand, if this same work were part of a golf course, park or playground, the "A" could be used since these type of "fixed works" are specifically listed under the definition of a general engineering contractor (B&P Code Section 7056).

Q: We've had an "A" license for many years. We have been told that an upcoming renovation job on a public facility needs a "B" classification. Isn't the General Engineering class on top of the 'food chain' so we can handle most any project?

A: The "A" classification is certainly the real 'deal'; however, it cannot 'trump' a "B" license. In order to work on the type of structure you described a General Building license would definitely be required. The "B" properly handles tenant improvements, including plumbing, framing, electrical and HVAC. The "A" generally covers heavy construction and fixed works including highways, power facilities, sewer and water projects, etc. The "B" builds structures for the "support, shelter and enclosure of people".

Q: I hold a "B" license; however, much of my recent work has been industrial construction. Do you recommend that I apply for an "A" classification?

A: Yes, securing the General Engineering class would be advisable. By definition, an "A" contractor's business is in connection with…"refineries, chemical plants and similar industrial plants requiring specialized engineering knowledge and skill…" Your industrial piping and other mechanical contracting would certainly fall within this classification. This is not to say that a "B" cannot build or work on some industrial facilities however, in my opinion, the "A" would be more proper.

Q: I have a simple question that I hope has a simple answer: Can an "A" contractor perform underground utility work—including electrical conduits. A city building department is telling us that our company must also hold the "C-10" classification.

A: Your question is a common one. Unfortunately some awarding authorities are not as knowledgeable as they should be regarding contractor license classifications. I'm reminded of the school district that improperly disqualified a C-10 (electrical) contractor who was low bidder on a communication-wiring project. They said only a C-7 (low voltage) contractor could do the work.

In your case, the "A" classification is certainly proper to handle underground utility work. According to the CSLB this includes installing electrical conduit or wiring under streets and roadways. The city would be correct in stating that a "C-10" contractor can perform this portion of the project; however, this in no way precludes the "A" from handling the installation (either directly or through a licensed sub). General Engineering contractors can legally build entire power (and other utility) plants; install pipelines for the transmission of electricity, gas and water; handle street and railroad signals; and perform the related trenching, grading and surfacing work.

Q: I have been the president and RMO of my company for 15 years (Class B only). During this time we have performed over 100 projects ranging in size up to $15 million. The vast majority of these projects have included work that, were it not part of a building project, would require an 'A' license: grading/paving, underground utilities, retaining walls, etc. Does my experience in managing such projects entitle me to a waiver of the "A" exam?

A: Based on our discussion and my research, it appears you would be eligible for the "A" classification and should be granted an exam waiver by the CSLB. Section 7065.3 allows the Registrar of Contractors to issue a waiver of the trade test if 7 specific criteria are met. First, you certainly meet the primary requirement having been listed as a member of the license personnel for "5 of the 7 years immediately preceding the application". Second, the CSLB has determined that the "A" and "B" are closely enough related to consider a waiver. Third, your background would appear to show that you have the requisite experience to qualify for this classification.

To secure a waiver, you must apply for an additional classification. Applications for replacing the qualifying individual will not be considered for a waiver under this code section. The CSLB also requires much more detailed documentation, compared with those applicants who are sitting for the trade test.

Q: I lost out on a recent bid that involved extensive electrical (C-10) work. I listed a C-10 sub but the apparent low bidder did not. Isn't there a law against an "A" doing electrical work?

A: An "A" (general engineering) contractor can properly handle the electrical work on any number of projects. This would include fixed works such as water supply, wastewater, sewers, refineries, transportation (airports, bridges highways), dams, shipyards, parks, chemical plants, etc. Since this work falls under the definition of a General Engineering Contractor (Section 7056 of the Business & Professions Code) the low bidder can choose to either self-perform or sub-contract the electrical portion of the project.

Q: A recent bid listed the "A" (General Engineering) classification to install underground pipeline for a sewer project. Shouldn't my C-34" (Pipeline) license also be acceptable?

A: A public entity can determine which classification is most proper on any given project. Often municipal governments and special districts allow more than one class to bid work. In this case the city may have determined that a "C-34" is too limited. It does appear the "A" is proper and the better classification for this job. Both the "A" and "C-34" can install pipeline as can the "C-42" contractor, if the project is related to sanitation systems. The work to be performed is a sewer project and appears to involve more than just underground piping. Street work will be required as will work involving a wastewater treatment plant. As we discussed, with your background, "upgrading" to the "A" classification would be advisable especially since you appear to meet the CSLB's qualifications for the General Engineering class.

Q: Can an "A" contractor do concrete work? If so, are there any limitations?

A: It depends. An "A" contractor can perform many aspects of the "C-8" (concrete) trade. For instance, an "A" can build culverts, set and pour curbs and sidewalks, and build underground concrete vaults for electrical and water projects. On the other hand General Engineering contractors should not be pouring a foundation on a residential property, building a patio, or contracting to replace a walkway at the local mall. Interestingly, since an "A" contractor can build a swimming pool, the related gunite and concrete decking can be included with this type of job.

Q: I applied for my General contractor's license a few months ago. Today I received a letter from the Contractors Board that says I am not qualified for a "B" unless I can show framing experience. They sent me a long list of trades. Do I need to show that I have done all of these? I tried to call the CSLB a dozen times but no one answers. Can you explain this rule?

A: There is no "official" policy that requires framing, however CSLB staff have decided that an applicant cannot qualify as a General builder ("B") UNLESS they have 4 or more years experience in framing AND several other trades. Officially, B&P Code Section 7057 only says that you must be able to show construction experience in at least two unrelated building trades or crafts. Even though you documented 6 unrelated trades such as plumbing, electrical, HVAC and carpentry, you did not specifically list framing.

Q: I am a general contractor and I have been having problems collecting payment on a job. The homeowner has been very slow on his progress payments and I am ready to walk. If I do this could I get into trouble with the Contractors Board?

A: If you are not paid for work that is performed, the law is on your side. However, I would not recommend walking off the job. This could backfire and you may have more difficulty collecting what is owed. Further, if you "walk", the homeowner could file a complaint with the CSLB that you have abandoned the job. Although there's a justification to do so, you could wind up with a citation—or worse.

To paraphrase attorney Sam Abdulaziz in his book "California Construction Law", the owner on private works of improvement must make progress payments to the prime contractor within 30 days after receipt of the request for payment unless this is modified in writing. If you're not paid on time, the owner is subject to a penalty of 2% per month, in lieu of interest. In addition, the prevailing party in litigation will be entitled to attorney's fees. Bring this information to the homeowners' attention.

Q: What are the steps to obtaining a general contractors license?

A: To secure a general contractor's license your first step should be to determine that you have 4 years experience in the building trades. This means having a background that includes framing, plumbing, concrete, roofing, etc. If this basic requirement is met, you'll need to file an Application with the appropriate state licensing agency. In California, this is the Contractors State License Board (CSLB). Someone who is familiar with your employment must certify your experience qualifications. A two-part exam will be required covering the law and building trades. After you pass these tests, a bond will be required as will a Certificate of Workers Compensation (or exemption if you have no employees). Fees to the CSLB will total $400.00.

Q: I am interested in pursuing a general contractor/builder license. I heard that it requires four years of experience in a related field. Does being a real estate agent qualify as a related field? If not, is there a similar career that does, such as a loan agent specializing in construction loans?

A: Being a real estate agent, loan officer, or working in a similar field would NOT qualify you to sit for the general building contractor's license exam. The State requires a minimum four years experience at a Journeyman or Supervisory level in the trade for which you apply. For general building, this means having management and/or practical (field) experience in at least two unrelated trades such as concrete, roofing, plumbing, plumbing, PLUS framing. You may be able to use a 4-year college degree in lieu of 2 years of work experience depending on the field of study.

If looking for a new career path you may want to try construction management or engineering. If your goal is to become a contractor, you could begin with an apprenticeship program. Good luck with whatever you pursue.

Q: Can I do "dirt work" with my B license? I have the chance to sign a contract for a project that only involves grading, trenching, etc. Would this be legal with a general building license?

A: If this contract only involves earthwork, it would NOT be proper with a general building classification. By definition, a "B" contractor principally works on structures and, as we discussed, no structure is involved in this job. An "A" or "C-12" (Earthwork and Paving) classification would be necessary to handle this work.

Q: I would like help in obtaining my contractor's license for General, C-10, and C-7. I have 15 years experience in the electrical field. Please advise.

A: Thank you for the email. With 15 years electrical experience you should have no problem qualifying for the electrical (C-10) or low voltage (C-7) classification. Since you can only apply for one classification at a time, I would recommend applying for the C-10 first since low voltage wiring and hookups can be handled with this class. Based on your limited description of experience, I do not believe you would qualify for a General (B) license. The "B" requires a background in multiple unrelated trades.

Q: There is a contractor that holds a "C-10" license who is acting as a General contractor. Can he legally do this?

A: If you mean can a "C-10" (Electrical) contractor act as the prime, or "General", on an electrical project then the answer is YES. If you're referring to this "C-10" acting as a General on a building project (such as a home remodel) then the answer is NO.

I have heard from several contractors (or their attorneys) recently regarding what appears to be a growing problem: contracting outside of your classification. According to Section 7117.6 this constitutes a cause for disciplinary action. A painter, plumber, electrician or any other specialty that acts as a General building contractor is sidestepping the law

Q: I was told I need a C-7 or C-10 contractor's license. What is the difference?

A: While both licenses are for electrical work, the C-7 is limited to "low voltage systems that are energy limited and do not exceed 91 volts". These include, but are not limited to, telephone and cable TV systems, satellite dish systems and low voltage landscape lighting. A C-10 Electrical contractor can perform all the work of a C-7 plus nearly any other type of electrical installation, wiring and hook-up. It's really your call based on the scope of work you hope to perform.

Q: Can we replace the air conditioning units on a roofing project? We have a C-39 (roofing) license and the project calls for removing and replacing 5 large air conditioners. We have gotten mixed answers to this question and would like to know if we're legal working without the C-20 (HVAC) classification?

A: The answer depends first on whether the units are to removed and reset or if NEW A/C units are to be installed. If you're simply removing (and reinstalling) the units in order to put on a new roof, then the C-39 alone is fine. On the other hand, if you will be installing new air conditioning units, then this could trigger a need for the C-20 class. Either way, it is advisable to hire a licensed HVAC contractor.

A second issue is the relative cost of these two project components. As we discussed, the roofing portion of the project is roughly 80% of the overall cost. Therefore, B&P Code section 7059(a) would apply. The code states in part: a specialty contractor may take and execute a contract involving two or more trades, if the performance of the work — other than in which he or she is licensed — is incidental and supplemental to the performance of the work for which the specialty contractor is licensed. This is a good rule to remember…. but is subject to interpretation.

Q: Are we allowed to sub out portions of a project? We have a C-8 (concrete) License. Could we for instance contract for a job but sub out the excavation or forming?

A: Generally, the rule of thumb when subcontracting is that you may sub out any portion of the job that can legally be performed under your license classification. In your case, it would be acceptable to sub out the earthwork and/or forming to another C-8 contractor or a "C-12" licensee to handle the excavation and grading. You can take a concrete job and subcontract every portion including the rebar and finish work.

Q: I have a C-61 classification. I want to apply for a second C-61 class. Do I need to take another exam?

A: The C-61 (limited Specialty) classification actually consists of 30 different "D" or sub-classifications. These include everything from Pool and Spa Maintenance to Siding to Synthetic Products. Since you've passed the C-61 trade test, the CSLB will not require you to take it a second time. You must however; show 4 or more years of experience in the new classification and file the proper application with the Board.

For those with any other classification, please note that the CSLB has completely eliminated the C-61 trade test since it had no direct relevance to the classifications it purported to test for. In other words, since it was impossible to devise one test for 30 different trades, the exam was scrapped.

Q: Our license classifications are C-36, C-4, C-34, and C-42. We have done solar system installations for many years. Do we need to apply for the C-46 Solar or are we covered by our original classifications?

A: Thank you for your timely email. The opportunities created by the ongoing energy crisis have undoubtedly crossed the minds of many contractors. By definition, a C-36 contractor can "install any type of equipment to heat water...including the installation of solar equipment for this purpose". The C-46 (Solar) classification is much broader and includes (but is not limited to) "radiant systems, evaporative cooling systems with collectors, photovoltaic cells, and solar assisted absorption systems". Depending upon the type of solar work you perform, your present classifications may be fine. My recommendation would be to apply for the C-46 class and request a waiver of the trade exam

3

Misconceptions and Quirky Law

Common Misconceptions Introduction

Mis·con·cep·tion: a mistaken idea or view resulting from a misunderstanding of something.

One of the biggest misunderstandings is that a Limited Liability Company (LLC) can get a contractor's license in California. Even though the license application says (in very small print) that LLC's cannot be licensed, some still apply for this type of entity. Out of State LLC's experience the biggest problem since they must form a new entity to conduct business in CA.

The immediate follow-up question when I inform a caller about this is WHY? Why does the state prevent LLC's from becoming licensed? The basic answer is that the State legislature has never given the CSLB authority to license these types of entities.

I do not know of any other State that restricts LLC's from obtaining a license. California has even carried this one step further. The CSLB will not even allow a LLC to be the general partner on a license. The only acceptable way to include a LLC is to list it as the limited partner on a LP license.

Other questions answered in this chapter include: Should you remove yourself as an officer on a license even if it has gone out of business? Do I need to test in Nevada since I have a license in CA? Can I renew my contractor's license even though it has been expired for more than 4 years?

Quirky California Laws Introduction

California, we have a Problem! Well that's what prompted many people to contact me during the past two decades. There was the caller who could not renew his license because the Secretary of State had suspended his corporation. What's a contractor to do who incorporates only to learn that his name style is not compatible with CSLB regulations? Then there are the endless questions on why the State of CA will not license LLC's (when most every other state will).

Those pesky, sometimes quirky, laws that affect contractors can often stop you from conducting business in this State. Sometimes these are long standing regulations that are generally unknown to most contractors. Other times, rules are simply unexplainable like needing to list "framing" in your detail of work experience. This is required in order to apply for the "B" classification even if you handle 6, 8 or a dozen other trades

You can apply and transfer your individual license number to a corporation but cannot do the reverse. Add or remove a general partner on a license and the number is canceled. Add or remove a corporate officer, and the license number remains the same. Merge your business and you could find yourself without a valid license in a hurry.

Remove underground storage tanks and you will need the Hazardous Substance Removal Certification. Remove Asbestos, and you'll need an Asbestos Certification and registration with a second state agency. See my answer to a flooring contractor who just encountered mold on a project and wanted to know if there is a specific license needed to remove this?

Q: I am thinking of starting a new company with my wife as majority owner. We are interested in qualifying a Woman Business Enterprise (WBE) specializing in public work projects. How does one go about doing this? What information will be required?

A: There are several public agencies that qualify woman (and minority) owned businesses. For state contracts, your wife should contact Caltrans' Business Enterprise Program. If her certification is approved with the State of California, many local government agencies will accept this in lieu of their own certification.

Realize that the State is very cautious when it comes to certifying a contracting business that appears to have been formed simply to take advantage of the WBE program. For instance, they will look very closely at who qualifies the contractor license. If your wife is not the Responsible Managing Officer (RMO), you can just about forget making it through the certification process. As we discussed, even though your wife may be company President and own at least 51% of the stock (minimum requirements), she would likely not be able to show the necessary "day-to-day" control required by Caltrans.

The State program wants to see the woman business owner in charge. She will need to show control over most aspects of the business. If a new corporation, the State will look at where the money came from to establish the business. Her detailed resume will be reviewed to determine if she has the requisite experience to perform and/or supervise the trade(s). For instance, if applying for a concrete certification will her resume show that she has poured concrete, set forms, installed rebar, or supervised crews at the project site?

Have your wife review the WBE application and determine if she meets their criteria. If so, give it a shot. There is no fee to apply

Q: I am a general contractor (B) and have recently hooked up with a development group. We want to assign my contractor's license to the newly formed LLC but do not know the requirements and procedures. I was hoping that someone in your organization would have that information. Also, what "percentage of profit" from development is customarily paid to the owner of the license for its use? Thank you for your time.

A: This question may be the single most misunderstood aspect of licensing today, as I hear this from contractors, lawyers and executives regularly. The most important point of your question is the part you did not ask. "Can I apply for a new contractors license for my LLC?" The answer is NO. The CSLB will not license Limited Liability Companies. Your first step should be to form another type of entity such as a Limited Partnership or Corporation. Once this is done, you'll need to file an Application for Original Contractors License and file the appropriate bond and Worker's Compensation certification.

As far as a percentage of profit, what is customary is up to the parties involved. Please remember that as the RME or RMO you'll be responsible for the work performed and should be a full time employee of the licensed entity

Q: When someone applies for a CA contractor license it's issued to the individual, right?

A: Not always. It is only issued to the individual qualifier if the license is a sole proprietorship. A Responsible Managing Employee (RME) or Officer (RMO) must serve as the qualifier for a corporate license. If the qualifier leaves the license he CANNOT take the number with him. It stays with the company. A RME or Qualifying partner can become the qualifier on a partnership (general or limited). If this individual is a RME and leaves, the license stays with the business entity. If he is the qualifying partner, the license will be cancelled.

Q: We have a former employee who is working illegally. He has no license and is being paid under the table. Will the CSLB do anything about this?

A: Absolutely! The CSLB has an Enforcement unit that investigates complaints of this nature; however, it may take months before they can get to yours. I would recommend filing a "Hot Lead" with the Statewide Investigative Fraud Team (SWIFT). By providing specific information to SWIFT, the Board should be able to quickly respond and pursue this unlicensed individual. You must be able to provide detailed project information such as where he is working and how long he has been on the job plus a physical description and other identifying information.

When SWIFT catches someone working illegally, they can fine the individual (sometimes thousands of dollars) or, if the crime is severe enough, arrest him or her. SWIFT can be reached in Sacramento at 916-255-2924

Q: I was involved in a corporation that went out of business in 1993. Now, years later, I've received a CSLB notice stating that my current "individual" license is under suspension due to an old dispute with the corporation. A dispute I was never notified about, and was never in a position to respond to, had I been notified. How do I remove the suspension from my current license?

A: According to my research, the corporation had two judgments (in 1994) that have not been satisfied. Although this license expired in 1995, you are still listed on the CSLB records as an officer. You never dissociated from the license and therefore remain responsible for these judgments. It appears the CSLB finally realized the association and sent you a "Notice of License Suspension for Associated License".

At this point, your options are to either fully pay the two judgments; offer a partial payment that is acceptable to whomever is owed the money; convince the court to delay implementing the judgments (because you were not notified); or bankrupt the corporation (speak with an attorney regarding this option). Based on my experience, the CSLB will not lift the suspension unless one of these actions takes place.

An important caution to contractors! IF YOU ARE PART OF A CORPORATION OR PARTNERSHIP THAT GOES OUT OF BUSINESS, BE SURE TO REMOVE YOURSELF FROM THE LICENSE. Writing the CSLB a letter, or completing a "Notice of Disassociation" can accomplish this. If you remain on the license, even it is no longer active, you may be responsible for paying a judgment — or dealing with other financial problems — many years later.

Q: We want to apply for a "Blanket Payment Bond". This is needed so our company can collect more that the standard 10% down payment allowed by law. My attorney told me about this but I have no idea what all is required. Can you look into this for our company? Thank you.

A: Very few companies are approved by the CSLB for these "Blanket Performance and Payment Bonds". These bonds (usually over $1 million) allow a contractor to ask for more than the law allows on home improvement contracts. Section 7159(d) states that the down payment may not exceed $1000 or 10% of the contract price whichever is less. By having a blanket bond on file, you could for example, ask for a 50% down payment.

To secure this type of bond you will need to write a letter to the Registrar of Contractors giving him the reasons and justifications behind your request. The Registrar would then likely respond with a further request for financial or other pertinent information. Ultimately, if approved, the bond would need to cover the amount of all outstanding contracts your company has in California at any given time.

Q. We moved across town about 6 months ago. Apparently we did not notify the Contractors Board and just discovered that our license expired. Do you know why the Post Office did not forward our renewal application? What can we do now to get our licensed renewed FAST? We currently have several projects in progress so this is urgent.

A: Thank you for the phone call. Depending on whom you talk to at the Contractors Board, the post office does or does not forward renewal applications. I usually hear from people who have not received their renewal. I cannot tell you why some correspondence is forwarded while other important documents are returned to the CSLB as "non-deliverable".

Regardless, the CSLB's official position is that all contractors must notify the Board within 90 days of moving. It is the company's responsibility to file the proper address change with the CSLB. As for what to do with your present urgent situation, I suggest having someone personally visit Sacramento; pick up the renewal application; have it signed by the RME and an Officer; and ask that it be processed on an expedited basis.

Q: Our father had an individual license that was re-issued to his corporation. Now he wants the license back. His license number begins with a 2 and was issued nearly 40 years ago. Can you help with this?

A: While it is simple to have an individual license reissued to a corporation, the same cannot be said for the reverse. Once a sole owner license is "re-issued" to a corporation, the CSLB will not allow it to revert back to individual status. For your father to qualify a new individual license he will need to file an Application with the CSLB, pay the fee, post a new bond, etc. No exam will be necessary; however his new license number will begin with a much higher number. His old license (now with the corporation) which began with a "2" is unfortunately lost for his personal use.

Q: If I become the RMO on a new license what is my liability? Can I be held responsible for problems on the job and money owed by the company?

A: I am often asked this question and it is a difficult one to answer. In your case, financial responsibility is your main concern. Your ultimate "liability", should one exist, will likely be determined by the courts or through arbitration. Whereas, the Responsible Managing Officer's (RMO) "responsibilities" are detailed in Section 7068 of the B&P Code; "liability" is only addressed as it relates to the registrar refusing to issue, reactivate or renew an existing license or suspending a license for non-payment of taxes (Section 7145.5(a).

I can best answer the question by way of example. Let us say a year from now the company does a project and there is a dispute. Almost certainly, as the RMO, you will be named as one of those responsible. Let us further assume that the dispute ends in a judgment against the company for $150,000 (and for argument's sake the financial award is not further challenged). At this point, you decide to leave the license. Unless you or another officer personally takes care of the judgment or the corporation pays it (or there is a declared bankruptcy), you would be prevented from qualifying any new or existing contractor's license or even being listed as an officer. This certainly is a real "liability"

Q: We want to do business under another company name but use our same license number. Is this legal?

A: It's against contractor licensing regulations to use two business names under one license number (B&P Code Section 7059,1(b)). It is my understanding your corporation recently bought an existing company and that you would like to continue operating under their "well-known" business name. You can do this if you apply for a new contractor's license number. This entity would still be part of the existing corporation; however, you could "do business as" (dba) the name of the company you purchased.

One important thing to keep in mind: This is the same corporation. Therefore, all officers on the new application must coincide exactly with personnel on the existing contractor's license. You must list the same President, Treasurer, Secretary, etc. If, for instance, you want the new license to include one or two additional officers, these individuals must be added to your existing license.

Q: I am starting a corporation in California and plan on also doing business in Nevada. I went on the Internet and found there's a contractor's license with almost the exact name that I want to use. Can I use the name anyway? What do you suggest?

A: The use of a business name generally depends upon whether you're applying as a corporation or sole owner. While there may be 20 "Smith Builders", throughout California, there can only be one (1) "Smith Builders Inc." Corporate names are regulated by the Secretary of State's office in California (as well as Nevada). As long as a company remains in good standing, the Secretary of State will NOT allow another company to infringe on its name. In many cases they will not even allow the registration of a similar sounding business name in order to protest the existing corporation.

Nevada is a somewhat different story. The Nevada License Board will usually block the use of a name (regardless if a corporation, partnership, LLC or sole owner) if it's too similar to an existing name on file. Using the above example, the Nevada Contractors Board would likely not allow a *Smith Builders Inc.* if a "Smith Builders" already exists. I suggest you write a letter to the Nevada Contractor's Board to determine if they will have a problem with your soon-to-be-registered California company.

Q: Do we need a contractor's license to manufacture and supply products to a general contractor? If we also install those same products, would this change your answer?

NO! and YES! You do not need a contractor's license if all you'll be doing is acting as a supplier of materials. Business and Professions Code Section 7052 states "this (licensing) chapter does not apply to any person who only furnishes materials or supplies without fabricating them into, or consuming them in the performance of, the work of the contractor". In other words, simply delivering carpet, or tile or trusses or conduit to a new home site does not make you a contractor.

However, if your company contracts to install—either directly or through another contractor — the product, you have just stepped over the line into the "Contractor Zone"

Q: On a Joint Venture in California do all "partners" need to be licensed? Is the Contractors Board very technical when they review these applications?

A: YES! By definition, all entities in a Joint Venture must hold an existing California contractor's license that is active and in good standing. If an entity's license is expired or suspended for any reason whatsoever, the CSLB will not issue a license to the Joint Venture. One recent group of contractors had their application rejected because one of the entities had a "pending" workers compensation suspension. On another application the issuance of a joint venture license was delayed because a box was NOT checked on the Workers Compensation Exemption form. The signatures of ALL qualifiers as well as an officer of record must be correct plus the proper contractors bond should accompany the application.

Q: I would like to reinstate my contractor's license. It expired a few years ago and I want to start conducting business again. Can you help?

A: According to my research your corporate license expired 2 years ago. Normally this would allow you to simply "renew" the license by paying a delinquent fee. However, your license was revoked and the corporation is no longer in good standing with the Secretary of State.

It appears you had a civil judgment that was never resolved. Many times contractors will allow a license to lapse and will fail to notify the CSLB of an address change. If an issue or complaint arises (after your license expires) which results in an investigation, the Contractors Board will simply send correspondence to the old address. Whether the notice is forwarded or not the Board will proceed as if you had been properly notified.

The result of this revocation is that a disciplinary bond is now required. In addition, the CSLB requires that all judgments first be satisfied. Finally, to secure this—or any—corporate license, the company must be in good standing with the Secretary of State

Q: Can I renew my contractor's license even though it has been expired for more than 4 years?

A: YES! The renewal period is 5 years. Within five years you need only file a "renewal" application, pay the $450.00 (delinquent) fee for an active license and comply with bonding and worker's compensation requirements. NO test should be necessary. If a license has been expired for MORE THAN 5 years, you must file a new license application and retake the license exam. An exception is if you're listed on another contractor's license as qualifier during this time period.

Q: Someone told me that if I hire an unlicensed subcontractor I could be held liable for paying their worker's compensation and payroll withholdings. This can't be true?

A: YES, this is absolutely true. As a licensed contractor, you could be held responsible for all Worker's Compensation and payroll taxes for employees hired by the unlicensed contractor. For instance, let's say you take on a home remodel and hire a painter who is unlicensed. He in turn hires three workers, one of which falls and is hurt. If a worker's comp claim were filed, your company would likely be held responsible since it is extremely unlikely the unlicensed contractor carries the required insurance. But wait, it doesn't stop there it gets worse.

Let us further speculate that a year down the road, this situation is brought to the attention of the Employment Development Department. If they investigate and determine that no taxes were withheld (i.e. these workers were paid in cash), EDD could rule that your company is now responsible.

We of course are looking at a hypothetical situation; however, as a licensed contractor, do you want to take a chance on all the potential liability?

Q: I know the CSLB will not allow a LLC to become licensed. However, will they allow a LLC to be part of a Limited partnership? What about if the LLC is not directly involved but rather a part of another entity?

A: This is an often asked question but with a slight wrinkle. Because the Contractors Board will not license a Limited Liability Company (LLC), attorneys and tax specialists are always trying to find ways to keep the LLC involved while not running afoul of CSLB regulations. Basically, the only way a LLC can be involved with a licensed contractor in California is to be a Limited Partner within a Limited Partnership. Your proposal is for the Limited Partnership to have another LP as its General partner. This is fine except the Board will not allow a LLC to be part of the general partner—even in the second tier.

Q: We are registered as a Limited Liability Company (LLC). Does the company have to be registered with the Registrar of Contractors or just the individual? All contracts with potential homebuilders are signed under the LLC name only and this LLC is not licensed. Are these contracts binding?

A: Uh-oh. A Limited Liability Company (LLC) cannot be a licensed contractor in CA. The company that has the contract must also have the license in the same name. It is not enough to have an individual licensed. I am not an attorney; however, based on the above information, it is my opinion these contracts are not proper. I would suggest consulting with an attorney ASAP. I would also suggest that you apply for a license under a structure that is accepted in California, such as a corporation or general partnership.

Q: We have a problem. The CSLB will not allow us to renew our contractor's license until the Secretary of State lifts a suspension. Can they do this? This is the first I have heard of any problem with the State.

A: According to my research, your corporation was suspended about 8 months ago for failure to pay the Franchise Tax Board and failure to file an updated "Statement of Information" with the Secretary of State. The Contractor's Board recently discovered your suspension when they printed and mailed your license renewal application.

Your first step should be to complete and file a list of current officers. Second, you must pay all back taxes and formally request in writing that your company be "revived". This paperwork can sometimes be expedited if it's handled in person or sent via overnight delivery to Sacramento. Third, once your company is back in "good standing" with the Secretary of State, return your renewal to the Contractors Board with a copy of your "revivor certificate"

Q: If we knowingly do a commercial job without a city permit, are we in violation of CSLB license law? If yes, what are the consequences?

A: As stated in B&P Code Section 7090, if the Registrar finds that a contractor has willfully and deliberately violated any state or local law relating to the issuance of building permits, he shall take disciplinary action against the contractors' license. The consequences may be a citation, temporary suspension or (if serious enough) a revocation of the license.

Q: We submitted our license renewal to the CSLB a few weeks ago. The Board's Web site states, "The renewal application has been received but not yet processed". What happens if it is not processed by our expiration date next week?

A: Your license would be listed by the CSLB as "EXPIRED". Without a current, valid license you are unable to bid or sign contracts. Once the Board gets to your renewal application, it SHOULD be backdated and no 'expiration' will show on your license history.

Of course the problem is the time period that your license shows "expired" and how this might affect existing (or potential) contracts. Hopefully, your customers will understand that you're making every attempt to keep your license in good standing.

It is important that renewal applications be completed and sent to the CSLB soon after they're received by the contractor (this is typically 60-90 days prior to expiration). It is also very important to insure that all questions on the form are answered; it is signed/dated by the proper personnel; and the renewal fee is attached.

Q: We're a flooring contractor and just encountered mold on a project. Is there a specific license needed to remove this? What happens if this discovery is considered to be 'toxic?

A: I am not aware of any specific license or certification in California for removal of mold. A contractor's license would be necessary to handle any renovation work caused by the occurrence of mold. Testing should be done to determine if the mold is dangerous and should be removed in a safe manner.

On the legislative front, the governor signed a bill that became the "Toxic Mold Protection Act of 2001." The new act required that the Department of Health Services convene a task force, comprised of affected parties, to advise the department on the development of permissible exposure limits to mold, standards for assessment of molds in indoor environments and standards for the identification, and removal of mold.

As one of its first actions the Department of Health Services requested that the Division of Occupational Safety and Health amend its general sanitation requirements to provide clarification to existing standards. The new language reads: "When exterior water intrusion, leakage from interior water sources, or other uncontrolled accumulation of water occurs, the intrusion, leakage or accumulation shall be corrected because of the potential for these conditions to cause the growth of mold." Standards may eventually be adopted that require special licensing for removal of mold.

Q: Is there such a thing as a "temporary license' in California to just bid on projects?

A: NO, there is no allowance for a temporary license. B&P Code Section 7026 states in part that a contractor is any person who undertakes or offers to undertake or purports to have the capacity to undertake or SUBMITS A BID to alter, repair, add to, subtract from any building, highway, project, development, improvement. As indicated, bidding requires that you have a license number.

Q: I am interested in starting a business doing handyman type work. All the information I'm getting is that I need a state contractor's license to do this. I haven't had nearly enough paid experience to qualify for that kind of license. Is there any thing you can do to help? I don't want to break any laws or put myself, or any one else at risk. What do you suggest?

A: You must have a contractor's license to perform work over $500.00 — even "handyman" projects. If you do not have 4 or more year's full time paid experience in the trade(s) it will be very difficult to qualify to take the state license exam. I would suggest seeking employment with a licensed contractor to gain enough experience and then file your license application with the Contractors Board.

Q: We just filed Articles of Incorporation but they were returned by the Secretary of State's office. Attached was a note that said I was required to have the word "Incorporated" in the name. Is this correct?

A: Thank you for your recent fax question. I must admit I was a bit surprised that your articles were returned. However, after researching your situation, it appears the Secretary of State was correct. Some—but not all — corporations are required to use incorporated or a similar word in the business name.

Corporations that are personal names (i.e. John Doe); professional groups (like doctors or dentists) or closely held companies (less than 35 shareholders) must use the word "limited", "corporation" or "incorporated" or an abbreviation of one of these words. Your articles specifically state this will be a "close corporation", which is why your articles were returned.

Q: I've had a partnership license with my father for over 20 years. He will be retiring and I want to apply for my own individual license and use the same name and number. Can this be done?

A: The CSLB will not allow the transfer of a contractor's license number from a partnership to a sole owner. Once a partner leaves a license for any reason, the license is cancelled. Your current business name implies this is a partnership. To continue using the same name (as a sole owner), you should immediately do the following: file a new original license application; write a letter explaining the significance and family history of this business; state that you will be operating as a sole proprietor; and further state that you will IN NO WAY BE OPERATING AS A PARTNERSHIP. You will also need to pass the required business/law and trade exams.

Q: I'm in a bind. I incorporated a year ago but never applied for a new license. I did not realize that simply adding "INC" to my name would trigger this requirement. Now there's a dispute and I need to get this corporation licensed quickly. What can I do?

A: Unfortunately, even if your new license could be issued "quickly", it will not likely help your cause. Although I'm not an attorney and no one can predict what a judge will or won't do, he will probably not rule in your favor. You are licensed as a sole owner and not legally able to contract as a corporation. This alone, regardless of the facts in the case, may decide who wins this dispute. Nevertheless, to protect yourself in future contracts, I would immediately complete and file an Application For Original Contractors License. Send or hand-deliver your application to the CSLB along with a bond, workers compensation certificate and required $400 fee.

Q: I just had my license renewal returned because my business name was "potentially misleading". I did change the name of my company; however, the CSLB letter did not fully explain why the new name is a problem. Any ideas?

A: The CSLB regularly reviews business names to insure they're compatible with the type of business being conducted and not misleading to California consumers. For instance, under Section 7059.1 [Name Style (Business Name) Compatibility with Classification], the Contractors Board would obviously not allow a plumbing contractor to use "concrete" or "landscaping" in its business name. In all likelihood, they would also not allow a "C-5" (Carpentry) contractor (who can build wood floors) to use the word "flooring" because it implies he holds the "C-15" classification.

After reviewing your letter from the CSLB it would appear their problem stems not from a classification issue but rather from the implication that your new business name implies you're no longer a sole proprietor. Use of the word "Group" in your new business name may indicate to the Board that you have formed a partnership or corporation. As we discussed, since this is not the case, you must state in writing that you're still a sole owner and have in no way formed another entity. Resubmit your renewal with this correspondence and the Board should now allow your new business name.

Q: Our license application was rejected by the CSLB because they say we have different officers listed at the Secretary of State (SOS). I am sure the officers are the same as we included on our application. What can we do to prove this to the CSLB?

A: Whenever an application is filed for a corporation, the Contractor's Board routinely checks with the Secretary of State to determine if the officers are the same. In the case of a new company, where no list of officers has been filed, the Board will accept the application at face value. This is based on the applicant listing (at a minimum) a President, Secretary and Treasurer (CFO). According to my research, you have someone different listed as President (with the CSLB) and Chief Executive Officer (with the Secretary of State).

The problem is that the CSLB and SOS often consider the CEO and President to be the same person when in fact two different people may hold these offices. The Contractor's Board asks applicants to list a "President" while the Secretary of State asks a corporation to file their list of officers including the "Chief Executive".

This is a classic case of two different state agencies having their own rules and regulations and not working together on a common definition. As we discussed, the answer to your specific problem is to list both the CEO and President on your license application and include a short letter to the CSLB explaining that two different people hold these titles. I have spoken with the Board regarding this issue and they stated your application would be acceptable with these changes.

Important Contractor Information:

A question in this column a number of months ago dealt with licensing requirements for "construction management". A recent email asked a similar question: must a construction manager (CM) be licensed in California?

My standard answer has always been, in part, that it depends on the contract. Is the CM or project owner responsible for the subcontractors? Who does the hiring of subs: the CM or awarding authority? Who is ultimately accountable if a construction problem develops?

This topic took on a different focus with a recent news article that a "development firm" has been accused (and issued a citation) by the CSLB for "working without a contractor's license". Of course, the two sides (developer and CSLB) disagree over the definitions and an administrative law judge will likely decide who is correct.

It is significant however, that the CSLB has in effect put construction managers, "design-builders" and some developers on notice that a contractor's license will likely be required if they directly hire the subcontractors who are performing the actual work and are given ultimate responsibility for the work performed.

Q: As a General Contractor in California, can I, or my employees, remove floor tile that contains asbestos, without special Certification? There is about 100 sq. ft. of tile in this residence.

A: A contractor must be certified and registered with the CSLB and Cal/OSHA for any work that involves 100 square ft or more of surface area that contains asbestos materials. If the removal of asbestos involves less than 100 sq. ft. of surface area the CSLB does not require certification as an asbestos abatement contractor. However, you must still file a CARCINOGEN 'REPORT OF USE' FORM with the Occupational Carcinogen Control Unit at DOSH. You must also make sure your entire crew completes 40 hours of asbestos training (provided by Cal/OSHA). If you want additional information on this subject, please write the CSLB or Cal-OSHA

Q: Greetings. I'm a contractor with a C-20 and C-38 license for HVAC and commercial refrigeration. We are licensed as "XYZ Refrigeration" because at the time that was the main focus of our business. Over the years we have seen a large growth in the HVAC portion of our business. Sadly, It's hard for a person just scanning thru the Yellow Pages to figure out we even do HVAC. For advertising purposes we would like to have something like "XYZ Heating and Air Conditioning, a division of XYZ Refrigeration". Can we do this without starting a new company? Thank you greatly for any help in this matter.

A: In order to conduct business under two different namestyles, you MUST have two different license numbers. The first could remain XYZ Refrigeration; however, since you're a sole proprietorship, I do not believe the CSLB would approve the second name as proposed above. "A division of" implies you're operating as a corporation. You may however apply for a second (C-20) sole owner license with the name "XYZ Heating and Air Conditioning". This would help attract potential customers who use the Yellow Pages or rely on other advertising.

If incorporated, "a division of" for the second license would be acceptable as indicated in your question. I would suggest talking with your accountant and/or attorney regarding the tax implications of doing business under another namestyle or forming a corporation. I hope this information is helpful.

4

What's In A Name?

What's in a Name Introduction

According to a Chinese Proverb, "The beginning of wisdom is to call things by their right names". With contractor's licensing, call things by the wrong name and you may not even get beyond the application process.

What's in a Name or your license number? Plenty! For many contractors, the business name is very personal. Putting your family name out there for all to see identifies you with the work being performed. Quality construction means a favorable impression on you and your name. Sub-standard or poor workmanship and your name and reputation are damaged.

A Business name identifies the type of construction performed. You wouldn't use plumbing in your name if applying for an electrical license (not that the CSLB would allow this). Just as important, a contractor cannot use the word "Incorporated" unless properly registered as a corporation with the Secretary of State. If you decide to change your business structure from a sole owner to a corporation, it takes more than simply adding 'Inc' to your name. Want to use the word "building" in a business name? Read on to see which contractors are allowed to!

What's in a Name or your license number? Plenty if someone else is using it! Identity theft should not only be of concern to consumers but also to contractors. The danger is that someone else will use your license number and botch the job. That's when major problems can develop for the real licensed contractor.

Q: I applied for a new corporation license and the CA Secretary of State approved this name. We're going for the "B" classification.

The CSLB came back and advised I "cannot use the word windows in your business name in Section 1". The business name is incompatible with the classification you are applying for. Because you have filed for a corporate license, you have 2 options: 1) Change name to one that is appropriate or, 2) write "DBA" and add a fictitious name after the business name shown in Section 1. I do not want to change my name. What is the best way to proceed?

A: The CSLB has the authority to determine if a name is compatible with the classification being applied for. Section 7159.1(a) states that "a licensee shall not use any business name that indicates the licensee is qualified to perform work in classifications other than those issued..." Since your name style implies you hold a C-17 (glazing) classification, the Contractors Board can require you to list a DBA, or amend the name with the Secretary of State. I understand you do not want to change your business name; however, the CSLB will not issue your company a license number unless you do so.

Q: I applied for a general building license a few months ago and just received a letter from the CSLB that said I could not use my corporate name. They didn't explain what the problem was, only that I had to change the name with the Secretary of State or use a DBA. I don't understand how the CSLB can tell me I can't use the name I legally registered with the Secretary of State?

A: Although the Secretary of State allowed your corporate name, the CSLB is not required to accept it. In your case, the CSLB may have made an error since "carpentry", while handled under a "C-5" or "C-6", can properly be performed by a General "B". I suggest contacting the Board in writing; ask them to reconsider their denial of your name style.

Q: I sent in the paperwork to change our business name and renew our license. It came back with a letter from the Contractors Board that said we could not do this. It says we must file a new original license application and will be issued a new license number. Can you tell us why we can't change the name since all we're doing is adding the word "INC" to our existing business?

A: Contractor license regulations require that whenever a new business is formed, the new entity must secure a corresponding contractor's license. You presently have a sole owner's license and recently incorporated by adding "Inc" to your existing name. It does not matter if you add "Inc" or start business with a totally new name; the new license requirement stands.

When you submitted a renewal and name change form to the CSLB, they determined that rather than changing a business name, you had begun operating as a new company. They were correct in sending the original license application. As for being issued a new license number, this depends on the percentage of ownership you have in the new company and whether you want the sole owner license number re-issued to the corporation. If you own 51% or more of the new company, you have the option of completing a form to have the license reassigned. One caution: like another recent caller painfully learned; once the number is reassigned it cannot revert back to you as a sole owner. This contractor had his number reassigned three years ago; then decided to leave the corporation only to learn he was out in the cold without a number to call his own.

Q: I've selected a name for my new corporation but have no idea if it's available. Can you help me?

A: The only way to insure if a corporate name is available is to contact the CA Secretary of State. Unfortunately, unless you visit in person or contact someone who is tied into the State system, this can often be a difficult and time-consuming process. The Secretary of State does have a web site where you can download a "Corporate Records Order Form". If you were not in a hurry, this would be the way to go. Complete and send this form with a payment and you should get a response in a month or so.

You can also go to their web site and do a search; however, unless there is an exact match, you'll have NO assurance that the name is actually available. A similar sounding name may prevent you from using this choice. Before drafting and filing the article of incorporation, I would recommend reserving this name; a process that gives you 60 days in which to file your documents and know that the name is yours.

Q: I am presently doing business under my personal name. I now want to change this by adding a "DBA". How do I go about doing this so I'm legal?

A: First, I would recommend filing a "Fictitious Business Name Statement" with the City or County where you reside and/or will be conducting business. This is usually a one-page form handled through the Business License Section. If the name you want is unavailable, they will let you know. Once this name is filed locally, you will need to notify the State Contractors Board. Again, this is a one-page form. Unlike many local jurisdictions, the CSLB does not limit how many people can use a given name. For instance, a recent Internet search of CSLB records showed 20 active licensees throughout the state with the same business name.

Q: I recently bought a store from a bankrupt owner (including the business name). He now has a new contractor's license and is using the same business name—the one I bought! I wrote to the CSLB but they said nothing could be done. Some contractors are beating the system and I'm beginning to feel alone playing by the rules.

A: I can understand your frustration. A business name can be crucial since familiarity and reputation are important. Trying to stop someone from using 'your' business name, as you discovered, is not something governed by the CSLB. Local governments are primarily responsible. Each county regulates fictitious business names except for corporations, which are governed by the Secretary of State. Doing a quick computer search, I found a dozen licensed contractors scattered throughout the state with 'your' company name—or something very similar.

Now that you've incorporated, no one can contract under your <u>exact</u> business name. Adding the 'Inc.' makes your name unique. You may wish to check with your local county clerk's office to see if the previous business owner is properly registered.

I can assure you that most contractors are "playing by the rules". It's just that a few of the bad ones seem to spend a lot of time trying to "beat the system" which is unfortunate for all of us — contractor and consumer alike.

Q: I am presently involved with a project that is being performed by a corporation. However, I know for a fact that the license number being used is issued to the owner as a sole proprietor. Is this legal? Does the Contractors Board have a specific regulation that prevents this?

A: A very good question. Contractors MUST be licensed properly to sign contracts, perform work and, if necessary, file legal actions. Any contractor performing work under a corporation must be properly registered with the Secretary of State and have been issued the proper "corporate" license by the CSLB. The contract and business entity name should be consistent.

Section 7059.1 of the B&P Code states in part that "a licensee shall not use any name style which is incompatible with the type of business entity licensed." If a licensed sole owner contractor has signed a contract under his (unlicensed) corporation, this would be "incompatible". Should a legal dispute take place, the court would likely disallow any legal action by the improperly licensed company.

Important Contractor Information

What's in a name? Or your license number? Plenty, if someone else is using it! Identity theft should not only be of concern to consumers but also to contractors. The danger is that someone else will use your license number and botch the job. That's when major problems can develop for the licensed contractor.

How you might ask could someone contract under your license number? Wouldn't a prospective customer check that the license belonged to the correct company? The license is in your name with your address and phone number. The illegal contractor would not have the official wall certificate or pocket card and advertising with an illegally obtained license would be too chancy. Plus wouldn't the customer verify all information with the CSLB by phone or web site?

In actuality, license theft, like identity theft, can be all too easy. As an example, say that someone in Southern California does a name search of the CSLB's records. He finds an active "B" license of someone in Northern CA. He begins quietly advertising and his quotes are 25% lower than legitimate licensees. A homeowner, as recently happened in Sacramento, checked with the CSLB by phone and was told that the contractor's license number was "active and in good standing". The consumer, however, failed to check that the name on the license was the same as the person that he just signed a contract with. When the illegal contractor screws up, as they often do, the CSLB will first come looking for you—the legitimate contractor. After all, it was your identity (license number) that was used in the rip-off.

There is no way to fully prevent this type of fraud; however, contractors can protect themselves by urging that <u>all perspective customers check the CSLB web site and confirm the name and status of the license and the personnel listed on the Board's records</u>. Periodically check this web site yourself to confirm that your license is in order (including your bond and worker's compensation insurance). Under no circumstance allow anyone—even a brother, or cousin—to use your license number (this is illegal).

5

Bids & Protests

Bids and Protests Introduction

The lifeblood of construction is the BID. Most projects start with the act of bidding. You win some and lose many others. That's how the game is played. However, sometimes the game is not on a level playing field. Someone has bid improperly or with the wrong classification or maybe does not have a contractor's license at all.

Enter the Protest!

One questioner wanted to know what to do after signing a contract with a subcontractor who was unlicensed at the time of a (public) bid. A general building contractor planned on self-performing all trades; yet someone protested, because he failed to list a "C-10" subcontractor.

Callers will contact me to discuss these types of bid situations. Often, I end up telling them there is little recourse on public bids if the awarding authority will not honor the protest. Local governments, in most instances, have the final say. If they determine that a classification or combination of classes is proper then they're proper. The old adage about fighting city hall has never been truer than when it comes down to awarding a bid on a public works project!

Q: I was the second bidder on a public works project. The low bidder has a "B license but did not name a "C-10" (electrical) sub. This is a significant part of the job (about 22%). Do you think it's worthwhile protesting?

A: Your email does not indicate if this GC intends on self-performing the electrical work. I can only assume that is the company's intent. This being said, I would not protest the award. Unless you know for a fact that the low bidder has no intention of handling this work internally, I would move on to the next bid.

Q: A concrete ("C-8") contractor will soon be awarded a public works contract that involves several trades. The job includes concrete, electrical, plumbing and waterproofing. Wouldn't a "B" be more appropriate? Do you think we would have any grounds to protest?

A: The awarding authority determines the proper classification for most public works contracts. If, for instance, a city puts out a project for bid and lists the "C-8" as the appropriate classification, then they have already made a determination regarding this issue. In the specific job you reference, concrete represents over 60% of the contract.

A "B" could also handle the work; however, as long as the concrete contractor uses licensed specialty contractors for the plumbing and electrical, I see no problem with awarding the job accordingly (waterproofing can be done by the C-8). Even if they did not list these subs on the bid, it is unlikely the awarding authority will re-bid for this reason alone. Remember, they're the ones who determined that the job is significantly within the C-8 trade. I would recommend passing on the protest.

Q: I am a certified general contractor in Florida looking to bid work in other states. Is my license reciprocal to the state of Nevada? Please advise. Thank you for providing an excellent resource for contractors everywhere.

A: Thanks. I am sorry to tell you, that your license is not reciprocal with the State of Nevada. To the best of my knowledge, Nevada only reciprocates with three states, California, Utah, and Arizona.

Q: I signed a contract with a subcontractor who it turns out was unlicensed at the time of a bid (he is now licensed). I did not know this; however, it has become an issue with the public agency we have a contract with. Was I in violation of any state law? Can the public agency yank our contract because of this?

A: You were in violation of Section 7118 (B&P Code), which states "Entering into a contract with a contractor while such contractor is NOT licensed constitutes a cause for disciplinary action". Since nothing in the statute differentiates whether this was done knowingly or unintentionally, the CSLB could issue you a citation. While it's unlikely they will under these circumstances, the public agency in question could press the Board to take action. On most public contracts, license numbers are required at the "time of bid".

Most bid documents ask for the general contractor's license number as well as the numbers of all listed subs. I am surprised that the awarding authority did not ask for a license number or that an unsuccessful bidder did not protest the award of the contract. Your contract could be voided (6 months later); however, this is an issue to discuss with your attorney.

Q: When a contractor has his license revoked, what happens to the projects in progress? Is it legal for him to finish these jobs? What would cause the CSLB to revoke a license?

A: If the CSLB revokes a contractors' license, the contractor has either done something fairly serious (like abandoning a job, fraud, or falsifying a license application) or ignored an order of the Board (such as a citation).

Section 7090.1 states in part that the "failure to pay a Civil Penalty or to comply with an order of correction or to pay a specified sum to an injured party...shall result in the automatic suspension of a license 30 days after noncompliance". A series of actions then kick in whereby the Registrar must notify the contractor of the suspension and give him 15 days to contest the action. If no appeal is received and the license remains suspended for 90 days, the license will be automatically revoked. In some cases a contractor moves and never notifies the CSLB of the new address. The contractor may never realize that his license has been suspended and, by the time he does, it is too late.

A revoked contractor may not qualify any contractor's license or be an officer, partner, associate, director or qualifying individual on any active license for a "period determined by the Registrar" (at least one year).

The issue of completing projects in progress is determined by the Registrar's order to revoke the license. In most all instances the Board will require the revoked licensee to find a properly licensed contractor to finish the work. In a few instances the registrar's order will allow the contractor to finish work in progress.

Q: I am in a dispute with a prime contractor. I filed my pre-lien and have been waiting for payment from the general. This is a public works project and he has yet to pay me anything. I am becoming suspicious, so to protect myself, I filed a stop notice. The city wants to release some retention funds but will not do so until I lift the stop notice. The general will not say if he intends to pay me immediately what I'm owed. Suggestions?

A: This is not a unique problem. I have received similar calls over the years regarding retention funds, city projects and non-payments. As we discussed, the best solution is to sit down at a table with the general and city staff and simultaneously sign the release, retention payment and payment to your company. If the GC will not agree to this "arbitration", then your suspicions are likely valid.

Q: I was low bidder on a recent public works project. As a 'B' contractor, can I self-perform all trades? Someone protested, saying I failed to list a 'C-10' contractor even though we intend to use our own employees. What do you advise?

A: As a licensed General Building contractor you can self-perform or sub-out most all work and handle any percentage of work you choose. Since you'll be using your own employees to handle the electrical trade, there was no need to list a C-10 sub-contractor. This would hold true for most trades except fire sprinklers and water well drilling. You're required to either hold a 'C-16' or 'C-57' classification or list a licensed C-16 or C-57 sub. I would recommend immediately addressing this protest head-on by writing a letter to the awarding authority. Point out that the protest has no substance and attach a copy of B&P Code Section 7057 that defines a General Building contractor.

Q: I am writing this question on behalf of one of our association members. A general contractor has asked me this question regarding "liquidated damages". If a project is not finished by the agreed upon completion date, can the owner collect damages? He had heard that this was not legal anymore. Can you provide an answer?

A: Thank you for your question. It is my understanding that contracts often carry a provision for "liquidated damages" when a project is not completed in a pre-scribed timeframe. According to a respected lawyer I spoke with, the inclusion of a liquidated damage clause is still legal.

According to this attorney, a section of the Public Contract Code addresses this issue. There is a separate Civil Code section that deals with private contracts. In both, if the delays were the fault of the owner (or public entity) there likely would not be a claim for damages made against the contractor. In the private sector, a liquidated damage provision would only be enforceable if the original contract were judged to have been "freely and reasonably negotiated". Because many com-petitively bid public work contracts are not negotiable, it is difficult to rely on this "reasonably negotiated" argument. Liquidated damages are most often assessed on a daily basis, although, if agreed on by the two parties, this could be weekly, monthly or even hourly.

The reverse is sometimes true whereby a contractor is rewarded for completing a project early and paid a bonus for finishing days or weeks ahead of schedule.

I hope you find this response helpful. This is a very complicated issue and I would recommend that your association member contact an attorney to review any contract he has entered into.

Q: I do not know if you remember us, but approximately 11 years ago you helped our company in dealing with the CSLB.

I was doing a search of what the "A" license classification is allowed to contract for, because we are protesting a bid. I found your website and saw some interest-ing questions and answers and decided to write you also. I am hoping you can assist me with the issue below.

The issue is a bid package that involves demolition (mostly interior components) and asbestos flooring at a school. The contract was awarded to a company that only holds an "A" license and Asbestos Certification. We protested the bid award based on several issues. One was that a General Engineering license couldn't work in schools. The CSLB also stated this to us, but the district states that the "A" license can do work in schools and they have a legal opinion letter. This sur-prises us because this scope of work does not require specialized engineering skill and knowledge and the "A" license is for fixed projects only (not for dwellings with people).

A: I certainly do remember you. Based upon what you have stated, I cannot understand why the school district made this determination. The proper classification would be the "B" (general building) or "C-21" (Demolition) — NOT the "A". You likely have a good argument.

The issue however, is not whether the "A" can work in schools — they can. The issue is the type of work they intend on handling at the school. For instance, the "A" would be proper if the project called for paving parking lots or installing underground utilities or handling site work such as grading or excavation. The general engineering classification should not be accepted if, for example, the contract calls for building classrooms; installing HVAC; fixing roofs; remodeling bathrooms or interior building demolition.

The CSLB will back you up to a certain extent through Board Rule 834. This states in part: "A contractor licensed as a general engineering contractor shall operate only in those areas defined in Section 7056 of the code"

Nevertheless, in most instances the CSLB allows local governmental agencies including school districts, to have the final say on what classification is, or is not, proper. For all the rules and regulations on public contracts, this is one area where a local jurisdiction is rarely over-ruled by the State. I have seen numerous instances where local agencies have misinterpreted the statutes regarding which classification is proper or limited a bid to one trade where several would have been acceptable. You may also wish to also consult a construction attorney. Good luck with the bid protest.

Q: We have an upcoming bid on a public works project that includes some federal funding. We are licensed as a general contractor but require a specialty class for this one job. Our application has been filed with the CSLB, but will not be processed anytime soon. Do you think we should still submit our bid?

A: According to Section 20103.5 of the Public Contract Code where federal funds are involved, "no bid shall be invalidated by the failure of the bidder to be licensed in accordance with the laws of this state. However, at the time the contract is AWARDED, the contractor shall be properly licensed".

In your case, it depends how long after the bid date it will take for the awarding authority to prepare the contract for award. CSLB processing time fluctuates, however, I cannot recommend submitting this bid if the award date is in the next few weeks. If the award were 8-10 weeks down the road, I would say it's safe to submit the bid. It's your best guess.

6

Nevada & Arizona Licensing

Nevada & Arizona Introduction

Which States require licensing of contractors? Are the licensing requirements similar from State to State? For California contractors, applying for a license in Nevada, Arizona or Utah may result in a small bonus — no trade exam. These four states have a reciprocal licensing agreement that allows a contractor in one state to apply for licensure in another state and request an exam waiver. In NV, CA, and AZ you must have been licensed for at least 5 of the past 7 years.

The waiver option depends on the state and classification. For instance Nevada and CA will **not** waive the electrical exam but Arizona and CA will. Likewise for drywall. All four states will however, waive the test for general building and engineering.

Each state has their unique requirements. Nevada for instance requires a financial statement from an outside CPA as part of its 26-page application. AZ allows this information to be self-certified but mandates a Transaction Privilege tax number. CA has passed a new law requiring fingerprinting. Utah eliminated fingerprinting several years ago but retained their ability to request them on a case-by-case basis. All four states require certification of work experience.

For information on licensing throughout the country, refer to the special addendum at the end of this book

Q: My Company intends on applying for a contractor's license in Nevada. We want the General Building and General Engineering classifications. I understand there is a duel license with both. Is this correct?

A: As we discussed, Nevada will allow a corporation to apply for an "AB" license. This "AB" classification allows the applicant to apply for two classes with only one license application. In most all other instances the State requires a separate application for each trade.

To qualify for the "AB" license, a corporation must be approved for an "unlimited" bidding limit. This bidding (or contract) limit is based on the Board's evaluation of your company's financial statement, bank verification form, etc. As such, there is no way to know whether or not one or two applications will be necessary until a review by the Nevada License Board.

Q: My California-based company was issued a Nevada contractor's license last year. We have bid on a few projects but, to date, have not done any work in the State. We are now being told that worker's compensation is required even though we have no Nevada employees. Is this correct? Why would we need this coverage if we have no work in NV?

A: According to my discussion with the Nevada State Contractors Board, worker's compensation coverage is required for most all companies where a "qualified employee" qualifies the license. This pertains to both NV and out-of-state companies such as yours. Under the circumstances you describe, this worker's comp requirement would not be triggered if an officer qualified your license (president, vice president, secretary, etc.). Since you do not have any work in the State, you're only required to have a "minimum policy" (although "minimum" was not defined by the Board).

An option would be to inactivate your license. The upside is inactive licenses do not require a bond or worker compensation insurance. The down side is that you would need to pay a new fee and produce a new CPA financial statement when you decided to reactivate the license. This is almost a classic "rock and a hard place."

This worker's comp regulation has apparently been on the books for some time but was not universally enforced. The NV Board is now enforcing this code for all license holders who have the qualified employee. Of course, for contractors that are actively engaged in construction and have employees, worker's compensation would be necessary whether qualified by an employee or officer.

Q: What States have reciprocal licensing agreements with California?

A: Nevada, Arizona and Utah reciprocate with California. This reciprocity only applies to the trade exam and does not cover all license classifications. All fees and other paperwork must be completed in each individual state.

Q: I want a license in Nevada. I am licensed in California as a C-10 (electrical) contractor. What's involved in getting this license?

A: The State of Nevada has a twenty-six-page license application. Among the requirements is a financial statement that MUST be completed by an outside CPA. If you request a "bid/contract" limit over $1 million, the statement must be reviewed or audited. A statement stamped by your bank or financial institution is also required as are personal disclosure statements for all personnel. A resume and four notarized reference sheets are part of the application. The filing fee is $600.00 and the testing fee should run $150.00. If applying as a corporation, expect additional paperwork and expenses.

Q: How long does it take to get a contractor license in Arizona if you already have one in Nevada?

A: Processing time to secure an Arizona contractor's license is hard to predict since you must ultimately register with several State agencies plus their private testing service! Generally speaking, it should take between 45-75 days to maneuver through Arizona's bureaucracy. Part of the time relates to the Arizona Registrar of Contractors, which has a minimum 20-day review period once the completed forms are submitted to their licensing agency. You will also need to register with the Department of Revenue and (if a corporation) the Arizona Corporation Commission. Being licensed in NV does not reduce the time it takes to secure a license in Arizona; however, you may qualify for a waiver of the trade exam.

Q: Our CA Company was just purchased by an out-of-state corporation. Although we kept the same name, it is our understanding we must apply for a new contractor's license. Is this correct? If so what will be required?

A: Yes, an Application for Original Contractor's license must be filed with the CSLB. It is my understanding that the "new" company is active with the Secretary of State and the previous company was merged out of existence. My research indicates that the CSLB has been made aware of this fact and will not allow the "old" corporation to renew it license.

In addition to this Application, the company must file new bonds and proof of worker's compensation. These cannot be transferred from the previous license. I would recommend requesting **in writing** that the Contractors Board reassign your existing license to the new company. Make this request pursuant to B&P Code section #7075.1(c)(1). (i.e. the company has merged into the new entity and the new entity was formed to continue the business of the formally licensed corporation).

Q: We would like to bid projects in Nevada valued at more than $1 million. How strong do our financials have to be to secure this limit?

A: The NV Contractors Board has a confidential formula to determine their bid/ contract limits. Several factors are taken into consideration in addition to the financial statement. I always tell my clients to ask for the bid limit they want. Let the Nevada Board tell you if they have an issue with your request. For example, say you ask for $1.25 million. If the NV Board will only go as high as $900,000 they'll let you know. Also note that financial statements must be reviewed or audited for bid amounts over $1 million. A compiled statement is sufficient for bids under a million dollars.

Q: My Company is a general contractor that does work in Texas, and a few neighboring states. We want to expand our services. Do we have to get a separate license for each state that requires it, or is there such a thing as a nationwide license?

A: Unfortunately, there is no National License. You will be required to secure a separate license in each state where you intend on working. While some states have no licensing requirements, others have very strict guidelines and regulations.

Depending on the State(s) you want to expand into, the process may be as simple as filing a one-page business license form or as complex as completing a 25-page application.

Contractor's Note: For information on licensing throughout the country, refer to the special addendum at the end of this book

Q: I am applying for a contractor's license in Arizona. One of their licensing requirements is securing a Transaction Privilege Tax (TPT) Number. Is there an alternative to posting the required bond? Can the estimated tax be paid up front in lieu of a bond?

A: This is a very interesting question. Arizona does have an "Application For Bond Exemption", however, it is nearly impossible to meet the State's strict exemption guidelines. Specifically, an applicant would need to submit a "letter of good standing verifying timely payment of all sales AND transaction privilege taxes (TPT) from another state…". Since I am unaware of many other states that have a TPT, complying is difficult at best.

Nevertheless, the Arizona Department of Revenue has stated it is willing to consider another State's taxing authority (such as the CA Board of Equalization) for exemption purposes — even if sales tax is the ONLY one paid in another state.

Arizona will consider issuing a TPT number if the applicant pre-pays ALL taxes that will be owed. In many instances this is a problem since it's difficult to know the full extent of work to be performed. However, if you know your company will only be working on one job per year, and the tax owed can be calculated, this "pre-payment" might be a good option.

Q: I was told that Nevada does not require a contractor's license for Painting. Is this true? We are licensed in CA and want to expand into Nevada.

A: The information you were given is incorrect. Like California, Nevada requires painters (and most all other trades) to first be licensed before bidding or working in their State. For your information, the C-4 classification in Nevada covers painting, sandblasting and wall-coverings, as well as drywall and acoustical tile. Based on our discussion, it would appear your qualifier could secure a waiver of the C-4 trade test since he's been licensed as a C-33 in CA for the past 5 years.

Q: We want to secure a Nevada contractor's license to handle general building and concrete. We have a "B" and "C-8" license in California. We heard that two applications are required. Is this true? If so, how do we go about applying for these licenses?

A: What you heard is right on the mark. Nevada, for the most part, requires contractors to file one application for each classification. Whereas, in California, a contractor can have 2, 3, or even 10 classes on one license, Nevada requires a separate license number for each trade. In your case, it would appear that both applications might be filed simultaneously, therefore saving some paperwork. It also appears, from my research, that your qualifying officer will need to sit for the law test and both trade exams.

Q: I just formed a Limited Liability Company (LLC) and understand I may have a problem in California. Can we get our LLC licensed in Nevada, Arizona?

A: You should not have any problem in Arizona or Nevada (or most any other state for that matter); however, California will not license a LLC. On several occasions, legislation allowing the CSLB to license a LLC has been defeated. One of the stated purposes of a LLC is to shield its members from liability. The CSLB would argue that this is exactly what they DON'T want.

Q: I was told I could get around testing in Nevada because I am licensed in California. Is this true?

A: Yes, in some instances' this is correct. There is a "limited" reciprocity agreement between California and Nevada. Nevada will waiver some trade exams if the applicant has been licensed in good standing in California for 5 of the previous 7 years. In your case, my research indicates that you've been licensed for 4 1/2 years in the "B" classification. If you wait another 6 months to apply you should qualify for a waiver. On the other hand, this means your licensing will be delayed by this same time period. Is it worth a delay of 6 months or more to avoid a 2 1/2 hour test? Please understand that 'Reciprocity' only reduces the overall process a small amount. All remaining application requirements must still be met—including passing the business management test.

The Nevada Board will "consider" a trade waiver — on a case-by-case basis. Your request must be in writing and will need to show a broad base of experience. You also will likely need to show that you have attempted to pass the trade exam at least once, if not several times.

Q: We are a commercial contracting company that is based in the Midwest. We're going to be working in the state of Arizona soon and I am getting incredibly frustrated at the Registrars Office in AZ. What is the process for getting a license that is quick and painless?

A few additional questions: Why does the "qualifying" person (i.e. employee) take the test; why not the president of the company or an officer? Why do we need a tax bond and a license bond? We are only doing one small job in AZ; doesn't this seem a little ridiculous to do all this for 1 job?

A: During the many years I have been involved with the Arizona Registrar of Contractors, they have always had a very detailed contractor's license application process. In answer to your questions: 1) the qualifying individual CAN be the President, another company officer or employee. 2) The taxpayer bond is required by the Department of Revenue to insure payment of Transaction Privilege Taxes (TPT), while the Registrar of Contractors requires the contractor bond. Once you have a history of meeting your TPT obligation, they will consider dropping the bond requirement. 3) Unless your job is on Federal property, a contractor's license is required even for the smallest project.

As for securing this license quickly, the Arizona Registrar of Contractors has a minimum 20-day review period once the completed forms are submitted to their agency. Before you can submit the license application, you must be registered with the Dept. of Revenue, Corporation Commission and have passed the required license exams.

7

THE RMO & RME

RME/RMO Introduction

Other than a Joint Venture License, an individual must be the qualifier on a California contractor license. The individual sole owner, qualifying partner, or a Responsible Managing Officer (RMO) or Employee (RME) can qualify a license on behalf of the business entity.

Without these individuals, the license would not remain in good standing—or for that matter exist in the first place. List all the officers you want or file an application with a dozen limited partners. Chances are the license will be qualified by a RMO or RME respectively.

This chapter will answer many of your questions such as: How much is an RMO required to own? Can a RME qualify more than one license at a time? What happens after an RMO qualifies three licenses in a given year? Can an RME/RMO take the license with him or her after leaving the company?

Two questions in this chapter are among the most often asked: "Could you tell me what type of activities would be expected of me in this (RMO) position? What happens after a license is qualified by an RME or RMO for 5 years?

Q: I am in the process of replacing our RME who abruptly left and took his license with him. Can I still get a waiver if I have been the company President for over 10 years? How long will it take for the replacement to go through?

A: You're referring to the waiver provisions in Section 7065.1. The CSLB eliminated the waiver for some people but maintained the waiver for most applicants. 7065.1(c) applies to your licensing situation. It allows for a qualifying individual who is an employee or officer of a corporation — and is seeking to replace its former qualifying individual—to do so with a waiver of the law and trade exams.

The corporation must have employed the new RMO or RME in a supervisory capacity and the license must have been in good standing for "5 of the 7 years immediately preceding the application for licensure".

While your Responsible Managing Employee (RME) did leave the license, he did NOT take it with him. The contractor's license belongs to the corporation not the individual who serves as the qualifier. Your company now has up to 90 days to qualify a new RME or RMO (Responsible Managing Officer). During this time period, the license will remain in good standing assuming there is no other issue such as a cancelled contractor bond or suspended worker's comp. certificate.

Q: I am going to work for a company as a RME and was told I need to be at the job site for a minimum of 32 hours per week. How can I do this if the company has several jobs going at once?

A: You're referring to Board rule 823, which states a "bona fide employee" is one who is permanently employed and "actively engaged in the operation of the applicant's contracting business for at lest 32 hours or 80% of the total hours per week such business is in operation, whichever is less." If you're going to be a full time employee and will be supervising or managing construction activities, you meet the letter and intent of the law. The State does not expect one person to be on every job site for 32 hours per week.

Q: I've had my contractor's license for 5 years. Another company now wants me to be their RMO so that company can get their license. What liabilities would I have as the qualifier?

A: While the issue of "liabilities" is one I cannot fully address, it is safe to say that personal liability resulting from a contract dispute or workmanship problem would, in all likelihood, be determined after a legal or administrative hearing.

For instance, let's say you're the Responsible Managing Officer (RMO) on a project that has several subcontractors. Your company becomes embroiled in a dispute over payment on some change orders. The issue is not resolved through negotiations and the matter goes to court. A year later a judgment is entered against your employer. For whatever reason they refuse to pay and the judgment is filed with the CSLB. You, as an officer, could ultimately be held liable for payment if the judgment remains unresolved. In turn, this would affect all licenses you currently qualify.

I suggest consulting an attorney to see if a "hold-harmless" agreement is feasible. Keep in mind that even if the company shields you from liability, the CSLB can still hold you responsible. CSLB regulations focus on immediate "responsibilities" rather than future liabilities.

Q: I will be buying the assets of a corporation and want to get the license under my company name. Since the RMO will be the same person, can I change the name on the license to my new corporation or do I need to apply for a new license. What do you recommend I do regarding this situation?

A: I have received many calls and emails regarding this subject. Changing the name on the license will not accomplish your goal. Since you're purchasing the assets of the company, but not purchasing the entire corporation (i.e. stock, liabilities, etc.), you must apply for a new license for YOUR new corporation. This requires filing an application for original license, posting the required bond(s), securing a new certificate of workers compensation and paying the required fee. The fact that the RMO will be the same person has no bearing.

A common error that is made when a company is being purchased or merged into another company is the timing. If at all possible, you should have the new company in place and licensed BEFORE winding up or merging the old company out of existence.

Q: I have recently incorporated in Nevada and have filed for similar status in California. I have been a sole proprietor since 1988. What are the pros and cons of either filing for a new license number in the corporation's name, moving my existing license to the corporation, or becoming an RMO for the corporation? Would becoming an RMO be quicker? I am somewhat lost in knowing what direction to go. Any help would be greatly appreciated. Thank you.

A: Let me answer the last part of the question first. As the qualifier, you will, by definition, be the Responsible Managing Officer (RMO) for a corporate license whether you apply for a new license number or have your current number re-assigned.

The decision whether to have your sole owner license re-issued to the corporation is personal. The main "pro" is doing business under an older license number that shows you have been in business for 15 years. The primary "con" is that once you reassign this number it can never revert back to sole owner status. In other words, if you decide to shut down the corporation, the number will be cancelled and lost.

There is no time difference between reassigning and having a new license number issued. Answering "yes" or "no" on a one-page form will inform the Contractors Board of your decision.

Finally, although you did not ask this question, I am wondering why you incorporated in NV only to turn around and file as a "foreign" corporation in CA? You may want to consult an accountant, but I believe you must still pay taxes on the work you perform in the Golden State.

Q: I am the RME on a license and will be leaving at the end of the month. I intend on semi-retiring and doing some work on the side. I was just told by the company President that I might need to get my own license. I told him I have a license, the one he is using. Who is right?

A: As the old saying goes, you can't take it with you! Sorry to tell you that your boss is correct. Based on my research, "your" license belongs to the corporation you work for. When you took the test a number of years ago to become the RME, the license was issued to the company, NOT to you as an individual. When you leave, you will be without a license. If the work you intend on handling is over $500, you'll need to apply for a new license and will be issued a new license number. No exam will be necessary; however, you'll be required to complete the application, pay the license fees and post a contractors bond.

Q: I'm a sole owner and have a "B" license. It was qualified by a RME; but he left the company. How many days do I have to replace him? We also recently became a corporation. Does this change anything?

A: Both your questions are important. First, you have 90 days to replace the RME. After that time period, you may request a one-time 90-day extension or your license will be suspended by the CSLB. Your license remains in good standing for this time period even though the RME disassociated. You could hire another RME to qualify this license or take the license exam and avoid this problem in the future.

If you are now operating as a corporation, and signing contracts as such, you must reapply for a corporate license. The name you use for bidding, contracts, advertising, etc. should be the same as printed on your license. I would recommend that you continue using the sole owner license until a corporate license is issued.

Q: I was told to start over and apply for a new contractor's license since my RMO no longer owns any stock in the company. Can you tell me if this is true?

A: Based on our conversation, the bigger issue here relates to the fact that your RMO is also the qualifier on two additional licenses. If he reduces his ownership below 20%, he must either remove himself from your license or disassociate from the other two companies. Even if he leaves your license, you do not need to "start over". Simply file an application to replace the Qualifying Person. You keep the same license name and number. Nothing changes in this regard.

Q: Can our RME qualify two companies at the same time?
A: With few exceptions, the CSLB will only allow a Responsible Managing Employee (RME) to qualify one license at a time. One exception is if the second company is a DBA of the first corporation. Other exceptions are considered on a case-by-case basis.

Q: A Responsible Managing Employee (RME) qualifies my company's license. He is not working out, but I cannot fire him because he has said he'll take the license when he leaves. He dangles this over me and I feel like I'm being held hostage. Do have any suggestions on what I can do to resolve this situation?

A: I am sorry your qualifier is a problem. However, be assured that when a RME is fired, or leaves your company for any reason, he cannot "take the license". This license belongs to your corporation, NOT the RME.

Q: We have a license in California that is qualified by a Responsible Managing Employee (RME). Our RME is not a resident of California and we have no employees in the State. Do we still need worker's compensation?

A: A company with no employees in California is not required to show the CSLB proof of worker's compensation. An exemption form can be filed instead. However, you may need to prove that your "out-of-state" qualifier (RME) has worker's compensation coverage in his home state.

I had a similar question from a California company that wanted to know why worker's compensation was required since his company had a RME but leased all their employees from an agency. By definition, if the RME is a California employee, you're required to show proof of worker's compensation. He or she cannot be a leased employee.

Q: Do I need to renew my license so I can act as the RME for a new employer? Do I need to get my contractor's license so I can be a RMO?

A: There is no requirement that you have an active individual license in order to serve as the Responsible Managing Employee. There is no regulation that requires you to have a license prior to becoming the qualifying individual.

There appears to be a common misconception that in order to be the qualifier on a contractor's license, one must first be individually licensed or that an existing license be active and in good standing. If you want to be the qualifying individual on a corporate license, you can directly qualify without first securing a sole owner license. Granted, in this instance the license number belongs to the company—not the individual — so you may want to eventually apply as a sole owner.

In order to serve as RME, your individual license MUST either be inactive (or expired). Section 7068(f) states that except in rare instances, any person who qualifies on behalf of an individual or firm shall NOT hold any other active license while serving in this capacity.

Q: I have been asked to become the Responsible Managing Officer (RMO) for our company. Could you tell me what type of activities would be expected of me in this position? I have read Section 7068.1 (Responsibilities of Qualifying Individual) but am unsure how to comply.

A: This is an excellent question. B&P Code Section 7068.1 states that the qualifying individual "shall be responsible for exercising that direct supervision and control of his or her employer's or principal's construction operations as is necessary to secure full compliance with the provisions of this chapter…" As we discussed, your main question is what constitutes "direct supervision and control"?

Board rule 823(b) defines direct supervision and control as including any one of the following activities: "supervising construction, managing construction activities by making technical AND administrative decisions, checking jobs for proper workmanship, or direct supervision on construction job sites".

I believe examples of the above could include a combination of reviewing contracts; reviewing plans and specifications; holding regular meetings with your project managers or supervisors regarding your company's construction jobs; and regularly visiting job sites to inspect for proper workmanship. According to the CSLB, it is important that as RMO, you participate in the day-today activities of the company.

Q: We have been in business for twenty-five years. My father is the RMO, but wants to retire. Do you think I can get a waiver of the trade test to continue the family business?

A: It appears you're eligible for a waiver of the trade and law exam. Section 7065.1 allows for an exam waiver since you, as the new qualifying individual, have been listed on the official CSLB records (as an officer) for 5 of the previous 7 years. My research indicates that the license has been in good standing and, as we discussed, you have been actively involved in the company's construction activities.

Q: I am a licensed contractor. I have been approached to become the RMO on another license but want to keep mine active at the same time. How much of this company must I own in order to continue using my current license?

A: You must own 20% or more of each entity in order to keep your license active while serving as the qualifier on a second license. For your information, the CSLB will only allow a contractor to qualify up to three corporation or partnership licenses (plus their personal, individual license) in any given year.

Q: My Company has a contractor's license and we intend on forming a second corporation with the same classifications and same officers. Is there a difference between qualifying this license with a RME or RMO?

A: According to my research, your present license is qualified by BOTH a Responsible Managing Employee (RME) and Responsible Managing Officer (RMO). Each qualifies one classification. When applying for this second license, the CSLB should allow the RMO to qualify but will not likely approve the RME. The CSLB reasons that since a RME must be "actively engaged" in the operation of the applicant's contracting business for at least 32 hours per week, he or she cannot reasonably be expected to be similarly employed in a second company—thereby working a total of 64 hours a week. If the CSLB makes this determination, you may appeal their decision in writing. My experience is they will consider these appeals on a case-by-case basis.

California Contractor License
Classifications

<u>A</u>	General Engineering Contractor
<u>B</u>	General Building Contractor
<u>C-2</u>	Insulation and Acoustical Contractor
<u>C-4</u>	Boiler, Hot Water Heating and Steam Fitting Contractor
<u>C-5</u>	Framing and Rough Carpentry Contractor
<u>C-6</u>	Cabinet, Millwork and Finish Carpentry Contractor
<u>C-7</u>	Low Voltage Systems Contractor
<u>C-8</u>	Concrete Contractor
<u>C-9</u>	Drywall Contractor
<u>C10</u>	Electrical Contractor
<u>C11</u>	Elevator Contractor
<u>C12</u>	Earthwork and Paving Contractors
<u>C13</u>	Fencing Contractor
<u>C14</u>	Metal Roofing Contractor (No longer being issued.)
<u>C15</u>	Flooring and Floor Covering Contractors
<u>C16</u>	Fire Protection Contractor
<u>C17</u>	Glazing Contractor
<u>C20</u>	Warm-Air Heating, Ventilating and Air-Conditioning Contractor
<u>C21</u>	Building Moving/Demolition Contractor
<u>C23</u>	Ornamental Metal Contractor
<u>C26</u>	Lathing Contractor (No longer being issued.)
<u>C27</u>	Landscaping Contractor
<u>C28</u>	Lock and Security Equipment Contractor
<u>C29</u>	Masonry Contractor
<u>C31</u>	Construction Zone Traffic Control Contractor
<u>C32</u>	Parking and Highway Improvement Contractor
<u>C33</u>	Painting and Decorating Contractor
<u>C34</u>	Pipeline Contractor

C35	Lathing and Plastering Contractor
C36	Plumbing Contractor
C38	Refrigeration Contractor
C39	Roofing Contractor
C42	Sanitation System Contractor
C43	Sheet Metal Contractor
C45	Electrical Sign Contractor
C46	Solar Contractor
C47	Manufactured Housing Contractor
C50	Reinforcing Steel Contractor
C51	Structural Steel Contractor
C53	Swimming Pool Contractor
C54	Ceramic and Mosaic Tile Contractor
C55	Water Conditioning Contractor
C57	Water Well Drilling Contractor
C60	Welding Contractor
C61	Limited Specialty
ASB	Asbestos Certification
HAZ	Hazardous Substance Removal Certification

Business & Professions Code
Division 3, Chapter 9 Contractors, Article 4 Classifications

7055. For the purpose of classification, the contracting business includes any or all of the following branches:

(a) General engineering contracting.

(b) General building contracting.

(c) Specialty contracting.

General Engineering Contractor

7056. A general engineering contractor is a contractor whose principal contracting business is in connection with fixed works requiring specialized engineering knowledge and skill, including the following divisions or subjects: irrigation, drainage, water power, water supply, flood control, inland waterways, harbors, docks and wharves, shipyards and ports, dams and hydroelectric projects, levees, river control and reclamation works, railroads, highways, streets and roads, tunnels, airports and airways, sewers and sewage disposal plants and systems, waste reduction plants, bridges, overpasses, underpasses and other similar works, pipelines and other systems for the transmission of petroleum and other liquid or gaseous substances, parks, playgrounds and other recreational works, refineries, chemical plants and similar industrial plants requiring specialized engineering knowledge and skill, powerhouses, power plants and other utility plants and installations, mines and metallurgical plants, land leveling and earthmoving projects, excavating, grading, trenching, paving and surfacing work and cement and concrete works in connection with the above mentioned fixed works.

General Building Contractor

7057. (a) Except as provided in this section, a general building contractor is a contractor whose principal contracting business is in connection with any structure built, being built, or to be built, for the support, shelter, and enclosure of persons, animals, chattels, or movable property of any kind, requiring in its construction the use of at least two unrelated building trades or crafts, or to do or superintend the whole or any part thereof.

This does not include anyone who merely furnishes materials or supplies under Section 7045 without fabricating them into, or consuming them in the performance of the work of the general building contractor.

(b) A general building contractor may take a prime contract or a subcontract for a framing or carpentry project. However, a general building contractor shall not take a prime contract for any project involving trades other than framing or carpentry unless the prime contract requires at least two unrelated building trades or crafts other than framing or carpentry, or unless the general building contractor holds the appropriate specialty license or subcontracts with an appropriately licensed specialty contractor to perform the work. A general building contractor shall not take a subcontract involving trades other than framing or carpentry, unless the subcontract requires at least two unrelated trades or crafts other than framing or carpentry, or unless the general building contractor holds the required specialty license. The general building contractor may not count framing or carpentry in calculating the two unrelated trades necessary in order for the general building contractor to be able to take a prime contract or subcontract for a project involving other trades.

(c) No general building contractor shall contract for any project that includes the "C-16" Fire Protection classification as provided for in Section 7026.12 or the "C-57" Well Drilling classification as provided for in Section 13750.5 of the Water Code, unless the general building contractor holds the specialty license, or subcontracts with the appropriately licensed specialty contractor.

(Amended by Stats. 1997, Chapter 812 (SB 857).)

C-2—Insulation and Acoustical Contractor

An insulation and acoustical contractor installs any insulating media and preformed architectural acoustical materials for the purpose of temperature and/or sound control.

C-4—Boiler, Hot Water Heating and Steam Fitting Contractor

A boiler, hot-water heating and steam fitting contractor installs, services and repairs power boiler installations, hot-water heating systems and steam fitting, including fire-tube and water-tube steel power boilers and hot-water heating low pressure boilers, steam fitting and piping, fittings, valves, gauges, pumps, radiators, convectors, fuel oil tanks, fuel oil lines, chimneys, flues, heat insulation and all other equipment, including solar heating equipment, associated with these systems.

C-5—Framing and Rough Carpentry Contractor

A framing and rough carpentry contractor performs any form work, framing or rough carpentry necessary to construct framed structures; installs or repairs individual components of framing systems and performs any rough carpentry or associated work, including but not limited to the construction or installation of: subflooring, siding, exterior staircases and railings, overhead doors, roof decking, truss members, and sheathing.

C-6—Cabinet, Millwork and Finish Carpentry Contractor

A cabinet, millwork and finish carpentry contractor makes cabinets, cases, sashes, doors, trims, nonbearing partitions and other items of "finish carpentry" by cutting, surfacing, joining, gluing and fabricating wood or other products to provide a functional surface. This contractor also places, erects, and finishes such cabinets and millwork in structures.

The amendments made to this section in 2002 shall become operative January 1, 2003, or as soon thereafter as administratively feasible, whereupon the C-6 Cabinet, Millwork and Finish Carpentry classification shall replace the C-5 Carpentry, Cabinet and Millwork classification on any license unless the qualifier for the license has passed the C-5 Carpentry, Cabinet and Millwork trade exam on or after January 10, 2000, or held the C-5 classification prior to that date.

C-7—Low Voltage Systems Contractor

A communication and low voltage contractor installs, services and maintains all types of communication and low voltage systems which are energy limited and do not exceed 91 volts. These systems include, but are not limited to telephone systems, sound systems, cable television systems, closed-circuit video systems, satellite dish antennas, instrumentation and temperature controls, and low voltage landscape lighting. Low voltage fire alarm systems are specifically not included in this section.

C-8—Concrete Contractor

A concrete contractor forms, pours, places, finishes and installs specified mass, pavement, flat and other concrete work; and places and sets screeds for pavements or flatwork. This class shall not include contractors whose sole contracting business is the application of plaster coatings or the placing and erecting of steel or bars for the reinforcing of mass, pavement, flat and other concrete work.

C-9—Drywall Contractor

A drywall contractor lays out and installs gypsum wall board and gypsum wall board assemblies including nonstructural metal framing members, and performs the taping and texturing operations including the application of compounds that adhere to wall board to produce a continuous smooth or textured surface.

C10—*Electrical Contractor*

An electrical contractor places, installs, erects or connects any electrical wires, fixtures, appliances, apparatus, raceways, conduits, solar photovoltaic cells or any part thereof, which generate, transmit, transform or utilize electrical energy in any form or for any purpose.

C11—*Elevator Contractor*

An elevator contractor fabricates, erects, installs and repairs elevators, including sheave beams, motors, sheaves, cable and wire rope, guides, cab, counterweights, doors (including sidewalk elevator doors), automatic and manual controls, signal systems, and all other devices and equipment associated with the safe and efficient installation and operation of electrical, hydraulic and manually operated elevators.

C12—*Earthwork and Paving Contractors*

An earthwork and paving contractor digs, moves, and places material forming the surface of the earth, other than water, in such a manner that a cut, fill, excavation, grade, trench, backfill, or tunnel (if incidental thereto) can be executed, including the use of explosives for these purposes. This classification includes the mixing, fabricating and placing of paving and any other surfacing

C13—*Fencing Contractor*

A fencing contractor constructs, erects, alters, or repairs all types of fences, corrals, runs, railings, cribs, game court enclosures, guard rails and barriers, playground game equipment, backstops, posts, flagpoles, and gates, excluding masonry walls.
materials.

C15—*Flooring and Floor Covering Contractors*

A flooring and floor covering contractor prepares any surface for the installation of flooring and floor coverings, and installs carpet, resilient sheet goods, resilient tile, wood floors and flooring (including the finishing and repairing thereof), and any other materials established as flooring and floor covering material, except ceramic tile.

C16—Fire Protection Contractor

A Fire protection contractor lays out, fabricates and installs all types of fire protection systems; including all the equipment associated with these systems, excluding electrical alarm systems.

C17—Glazing Contractor

A glazing contractor selects, cuts, assembles and/or installs all makes and kinds of glass, glass work, mirrored glass, and glass substitute materials for glazing; executes the fabrication and glazing of frames, panels, sashes and doors; and/or installs these items in any structure.

C20—Warm-Air Heating, Ventilating and Air-Conditioning Contractor

A warm-air heating, ventilating and air-conditioning contractor fabricates, installs, maintains, services and repairs warm-air heating systems and water heating heat pumps, complete with warm-air appliances; ventilating systems complete with blowers and plenum chambers; air-conditioning systems complete with air-conditioning unit; and the ducts, registers, flues, humidity and thermostatic controls and air filters in connection with any of these systems. This classification shall include warm-air heating, ventilating and air-conditioning systems which utilize solar energy.

C21—Building Moving/Demolition Contractor

A building moving/demolition contractor raises, lowers, cribs, underpins, demolishes and moves or removes structures, including their foundations. This classification does not include the alterations, additions, repairs or rehabilitation of the permanently retained portions of such structures.

C23—Ornamental Metal Contractor

An ornamental metals contractor assembles, casts, cuts, shapes, stamps, forges, welds, fabricates and installs, sheet, rolled and cast, brass, bronze, copper, cast iron, wrought iron, monel metal, stainless steel, steel, and/or any other metal for the architectural treatment and ornamental decoration of structures. This classification does not include the work of a sheet metal contractor.

C27—Landscaping Contractor

A landscape contractor constructs, maintains, repairs, installs, or subcontracts the development of landscape systems and facilities for public and private gardens and other areas which are designed to aesthetically, architecturally, horticulturally, or functionally improve the grounds within or surrounding a structure or a tract or plot of land. In connection therewith, a landscape contractor prepares and grades plots and areas of land for the installation of any architectural, horticultural and decorative treatment or arrangement.

C28—Lock and Security Equipment Contractor

A lock and security equipment contractor evaluates, sets-up, installs, maintains and repairs all doors and door assemblies, gates, locks and locking devices, panic and fire rated exit devices, manual and automatic operated gate and door closures and releases, jail and prison locking devices and permanently installed or built in safes and vaults. This classification includes but is not limited to master key systems, metal window guards, security doors, card activated and electronic access control systems for control equipment, motion and other types of detectors and computer systems for control and audit of control systems and other associated equipment. Fire alarm systems are specifically not included in this section.

C29—Masonry Contractor

A masonry contractor installs concrete units and baked clay products; concrete, glass and clay block; natural and manufactured stone; terra cotta; and firebrick or other material for refractory work. This classification includes the fabrication and installation of masonry component units for structural load bearing and non-load bearing walls for structures and fences installed with or without mortar; ceramic veneer (not tile) and thin brick that resembles full brick for facing; paving; and clear waterproofing, cleaning and caulking incidental to masonry construction.

C31—Construction Zone Traffic Control Contractor

A construction zone traffic control contractor prepares or removes lane closures, flagging, or traffic diversions, utilizing portable devices, such as cones, delineators, barricades, sign stands, flashing beacons, flashing arrow trailers, and changeable message signs, on roadways, including, but not limited to, public streets, highways, or any public conveyance.

C32—Parking and Highway Improvement Contractor

A parking and highway improvement contractor applies and installs protective coatings, vehicle stops, guard rails and mechanical devices, directional lines, buttons, markers, signs and arrows on the horizontal surface of any game court, parking facility, airport, highway or roadway constructed of concrete, asphalt or similar material. This classification includes the surface preparatory work necessary for the application of protective coatings but does not include the re-paving of these surfaces.

C33—Painting and Decorating Contractor

A painting and decorating contractor prepares by scraping, sandblasting or other means and applies any of the following: paints, papers, textures, fabrics, pigments, oils, turpentines, japans, driers, thinners, varnishes, shellacs, stains, fillers, waxes, adhesives, water and any other vehicles, mediums and materials which adhere by evaporation and may be mixed, used and applied to the surfaces of structures and the appurtenances thereto for purposes of decorating, protecting, fireproofing and waterproofing.

C34—Pipeline Contractor

A pipeline contractor fabricates and installs pipelines for the conveyance of fluids, such as water, gas, or petroleum, or for the containment or protection of any other material, including the application of protective coatings or systems and the trenching, boring, shoring, backfilling, compacting, paving and surfacing necessary to complete the installation of such pipelines.

C35—Lathing and Plastering Contractor

(a) A lathing and plastering contractor coats surfaces with a mixture of sand, gypsum plaster, quick-lime or hydrated lime and water, or sand and cement and water, or a combination of such other materials that create a permanent surface coating, including coatings for the purpose of soundproofing and fireproofing. These coatings are applied with a plasterer's trowel or sprayed over any surface that offers a mechanical means for the support of such coating, and will adhere by suction. This contractor also installs lath (including metal studs) or any other material prepared or manufactured to provide a base or bond for such coating.

(b) A lathing and plastering contractor also applies and affixes wood and metal lath, or any other material prepared or manufactured to provide key or suction bases for the support of plaster coatings. This classification includes the channel work and metal studs for the support of metal or any other lathing material and for solid plaster partitions.

C36—Plumbing Contractor

A plumbing contractor provides a means for a supply of safe water, ample in volume and of suitable temperature for the purpose intended and the proper disposal of fluid waste from the premises in all structures and fixed works. This classification includes but is not limited to:

(a) Complete removal of waste from the premises or the construction and connection of on-site waste disposal systems;

(b) Piping, storage tanks and venting for a safe and adequate supply of gases and liquids for any purpose, including vacuum, compressed air and gases for medical, dental, commercial and industrial uses;

(c) All gas appliances, flues and gas connections for all systems including suspended space heating units. This does not include forced warm air units;

(d) Water and gas piping from the property owner's side of the utility meter to the structure or fixed works;

(e) Installation of any type of equipment to heat water, or fluids, to a temperature suitable for the purposes listed in this section, including the installation of solar equipment for this purpose; and

(f) The maintenance and replacement of all items described above and all health and safety devices such as, but not limited to, gas earthquake valves, gas control valves, back flow preventors, water conditioning equipment and regulating valves.

C38—Refrigeration Contractor

A refrigeration contractor constructs, fabricates, erects, installs, maintains, services and repairs refrigerators, refrigerated rooms, and insulated refrigerated spaces, temperature insulation, air-conditioning units, ducts, blowers, registers, humidity and thermostatic controls for the control of air, liquid, and/or gas temperatures below fifty degrees Fahrenheit (50), or ten degrees Celsius (10).

C39—Roofing Contractor

A roofing contractor installs products and repairs surfaces that seal, waterproof and weatherproof structures. This work is performed to prevent water or its derivatives, compounds or solids from penetrating such protection and gaining access to material or space beyond. In the course of this work, the contractor examines and/or prepares surfaces and uses the following material: asphaltum, pitch, tar, felt, glass fabric, urethane foam, metal roofing systems, flax, shakes, shingles, roof tile, slate or any other roofing, waterproofing, weatherproofing or membrane material(s) or a combination thereof.

C42—Sanitation System Contractor

A sanitation system contractor fabricates and installs cesspools, septic tanks, storm drains, and other sewage disposal and drain structures. This classification includes the laying of cast-iron, steel, concrete, vitreous and nonvitreous pipe and any other hardware associated with these systems.

C43—Sheet Metal Contractor

A sheet metal contractor selects, cuts, shapes, fabricates and installs sheet metal such as cornices, flashings, gutters, leaders, pans, kitchen equipment, duct work (including insulation, patented chimneys, metal flues, metal roofing systems and any other installations requiring sheet metal).

C45—Electrical Sign Contractor

An electrical sign contractor fabricates, installs and erects electrical signs, including the wiring of such electrical signs.

C46—Solar Contractor

A solar contractor installs, modifies, maintains, and repairs active solar energy systems. An active solar energy system consists of components that are thermally isolated from the living space for collection of solar energy and transfer of thermal energy to provide electricity and/or heating and cooling of air or water. Active solar energy systems include, but are not limited to, forced air systems, forced circulation water systems, thermosiphon systems, integral collector/storage systems, radiant systems, evaporative cooling systems with collectors, regenerative rockbed cooling systems, photovoltaic cells, and solar assisted absorption cooling systems.

A licensee classified in this section shall not undertake or perform building or construction trades, crafts or skills, except when required to install an active solar energy system. The C-46 classification will be issued after development of an examination. (Note: Development of the examination has been completed.)

C47—Manufactured Housing Contractor

(a) A general manufactured housing contractor installs, alters, repairs or prepares for moving any type of manufactured housing as that term is defined in Section 18007 of the Health and Safety Code, including the accessory buildings or structures, and the foundations. A manufactured house does not include any recreational vehicle, commercial coach or factory built housing as that term is defined in Section 19971 of the Health and Safety Code.

(b) A general manufactured housing contractor may provide utility services on a single-family individual site placement. Utility services mean the connection of gas, water, sewer and electrical utilities to the home.

C50—Reinforcing Steel Contractor

A reinforcing steel contractor fabricates, places and ties steel mesh or steel reinforcing bars (rods), of any profile, perimeter, or cross-section that are or may be used to reinforce concrete structures.

C51—Structural Steel Contractor

A structural steel contractor fabricates and erects structural steel shapes and plates, of any profile, perimeter or cross-section, that are or may be used as structural members for buildings and structures, including the riveting, welding, rigging and metal roofing systems necessary to perform this work.

C53—Swimming Pool Contractor

A swimming pool contractor constructs swimming pools, spas or hot tubs, including installation of solar heating equipment using those trades or skills necessary for such construction.

C54—Ceramic and Mosaic Tile Contractor

A ceramic and mosaic tile contractor prepares surfaces as necessary and installs glazed wall, ceramic, mosaic, quarry, paver, faience, glass mosaic and stone tiles; thin tile that resembles full brick, natural or simulated stone slabs for bathtubs, showers and horizontal surfaces inside of buildings, or any tile units set in the traditional or innovative tile methods, excluding hollow or structural partition tile.

C55—Water Conditioning Contractor

A water conditioning contractor installs water conditioning equipment with the use of only such pipe and fittings as are necessary to connect the water conditioning equipment to the water supply system and to by-pass all those parts of the water supply system within the premises from which conditioned water is to be excluded.

C57—Water Well Drilling Contractor

A well drilling contractor installs and repairs water wells and pumps by boring, drilling, excavating, casing, cementing and cleaning to provide a supply of uncontaminated water.

C60—Welding Contractor

A welding contractor causes metals to become permanently attached, joined and fabricated by the use of gases and electrical energy, which creates temperatures of sufficient heat to perform this work.

C61—Limited Specialty

(a) Limited specialty is a specialty contractor classification limited to a field and scope of operations of specialty contracting for which an applicant is qualified other than any of the specialty contractor classifications listed and defined in this article.

(b) An applicant classified and licensed in the classification Limited Specialty shall confine activities as a contractor to that field or fields and scope of operations set forth in the application and accepted by the Registrar or to that permitted by Section 831.

(c) Upon issuance of a C-61 license, the Registrar shall endorse upon the face of the original license certificate the field and scope of operations in which the licensee has demonstrated qualifications.

(d) A specialty contractor, other than a C-61 contractor, may perform work within the field and scope of the operations of Classification C-61, provided the work is consistent with established usage and procedure in the construction industry and is related to the specialty contractor's classification.

The CSLB has listed the C-61 classification into "D" categories for administrative tracking. See list below.

D03—Awnings
D04—Central Vacuum Systems
D06—Concrete Related Services
D09—Drilling, Blasting and Oil Field Work
D10—Elevated Floors
D12—Synthetic Products
D16—Hardware, Locks and Safes
D21—Machinery and Pumps
D24—Metal Products
D28—Doors, Gates and Activating Devices
D29—Paperhanging
D30—Pile Driving and Pressure Foundation Jacking
D31—Pole Installation and Maintenance
D34—Prefabricated Equipment
D35—Pool and Spa Maintenance
D38—Sand and Water Blasting
D39—Scaffolding
D40—Service Station Equipment and Maintenance
D41—Siding and Decking
D42—Sign Installation
D49—Tree Service
D50—Suspended Ceilings
D52—Window Coverings
D53—Wood Tanks
D56—Trenching Only
D59—Hydroseed Spraying
D62—Air and Water Balancing
D63—Construction Clean-up
D64—Non-specialized
D65—Weatherization and Energy Conservation

ASB—Asbestos Certification

7058.5. (a) No contractor shall engage in asbestos-related work, as defined in Section 6501.8 of the Labor Code, which involves 100 square feet or more of surface area of asbestos containing materials, unless the qualifier for the license passes an asbestos certification examination.

No asbestos certification examination shall be required for contractors involved with the installation, maintenance, and repair of asbestos cement pipe or sheets, vinyl asbestos floor materials, or asbestos bituminous or resinous materials.

"Asbestos" as used in this section, has the same meaning as defined in Section 6501.7 of the Labor Code.

HAZ—Hazardous Substance Removal Certification

7058.7. (a) No contractor shall engage in a removal or remedial action, as defined in subdivision (d), unless the qualifier for the license has passed an approved hazardous substance certification examination.

(b) (1) The Contractors' State License Board, the Division of Occupational Safety and Health of the Department of Industrial Relations, and the Department of Toxic Substances Control shall jointly select an advisory committee, which shall be composed of two representatives of hazardous substance removal workers in California, two general engineering contractors in California, and two representatives of insurance companies in California who shall be selected by the Insurance Commissioner.

(d) For purposes of this section "removal or remedial action" has the same meaning as found in Chapter 6.8 (commencing with Section 25300) of Division 20 of the Health and Safety Code, if the action requires the contractor to dig into the surface of the earth and remove the dug material and the action is at a site listed pursuant to Section 25356 of the Health and Safety Code or any other site listed as a hazardous waste site by the Department of Toxic Substances Control or a site listed on the National Priorities List compiled pursuant to the Comprehensive Environmental Response, Compensation, and Liability Act of 1980 (42 U.S.C. Sec. 9601 et seq.). "Removal or remedial action" does not include asbestos-related work, as defined in Section 6501.8 of the Labor Code, or work related to a hazardous substance spill on a highway.

(e) (1) A contractor shall not install or remove an underground storage tank, unless the contractor has passed the hazardous substance certification examination developed pursuant to this section.

(2) A contractor who is not certified may bid on or contract for the installation or removal of an underground tank, as long as the work is performed by a contractor who is certified pursuant to this section.

(3) For purposes of this subdivision, "underground storage tank" has the same meaning as defined in subdivision (x) of Section 25281 of the Health and Safety Code.

50-State Licensing Information

Disclaimer: The following information is provided as a basic informational guide to contractors licensing in the United States. The reader is cautioned that recent changes to state laws or regulations can impact licensing requirements in a given State. It is recommended that you confirm all licensing requirements prior to contracting in a State. For detailed information on how to become licensed in a State, you should contact the state directly via phone, mail or through their website.

Your feedback and comments regarding this 50-State licensing section are appreciated. Please e-mail comments to: info@cutredtape.com.

Alabama
The State licenses and regulates commercial/industrial contractors in the major and specialty classifications that constitute the industry.

General Contractors Board
2525 Fairlane Drive
Montgomery, AL 36116
(334) 272-5030
www.genconbd.state.al.us

Alaska
General, Specialty and Mechanical Contractors License Required

Division of Occupational Licensing
Box 110806
Juneau, AK 99811-0806
(907) 465-8443
 http://www.dced.state.ak.us/occ/pcon.htm

Arizona
Commercial and Residential Contractors License required for general and most all trades

Arizona Registrar of Contractors
800 W. Washington, 6th Floor
Phoenix, AZ 85007
(602) 542-1525
www.rc.state.az.us

Arkansas
Commercial Contractors License Required.

Contractors License Board
4100 Richards Road
North Little Rock, AR 72117
(501) 372-4661
www.state.ar.us/clb

California
Contractors License required for all trades

Contractors State License Board
P.O. box 2600
Sacramento, CA 95826
(916) 255-3900
www.cslb.ca.gov

Colorado
State license required for electrical, asbestos removal, plumbers, and pesticides trades. For all other licensing, please contact the local government office where you plan to contract.

Division of Registrations
1560 Broadway, Suite 1300
Denver, CO 80202
303-894-7690
www.dora.state.co.us/registrations/index.htm

Connecticut
License required for electrical and plumbing trades. For all other licensing, please contact the local government office where you plan to contract.

Department of Consumer Protection
License Services Division
165 Capitol Avenue
Hartford, CT 06106
860-713-6135
www.dcp.state.ct.us/licensing/

Delaware

Delaware Water Well Contractors Licensing Board
www.dnrec.state.de.us/dnrec2000/
Other Business Licensing
www.state.de.us/revenue

District of Columbia
No information available.

Florida
Contractors license required for general contracting and most specialty trades.

Dept. of Business and Professional Regulation
1940 N. Monroe
Tallahassee, FL 3299-0783
850-487-1395
www.state.fl.us/dbpr/pro/cilb/cilb_index.shtml

Georgia
State license is required for Air Conditioning, Electrical, and Plumbing trades. For all other trades contact the local government where you intend to contract.

Construction Industry Board
237 Coliseum Drive
Macon, GA 31217
478-207-1416
www.sos.state.ga.us/plb/construct

Hawaii
Contractors license required for general contracting and most specialty trades.

Department of Commerce & Consumer Affairs
Division of Profession & Vocational Licensing
335 Merchant Street
Honolulu, HI 96801
808-586-3000
www.state.hi.us/dcca/pvl

Idaho
License required for electrical, plumbing, pesticide, manufactured housing, landscape architecture, and asbestos removal. No state license for general contracting at this time.

Division of Building Safety
1090 East Watertower Street
Meriman, ID 83642
208-334-3950
http://www2.state.id.us/dbs

Illinois
State license required for roofing. No state license for general contracting at this time.

Department of Professional Regulation
320 W. Washington Street
Springfield, IL 62786
217-785-0800
www.dpr.state.il.us

Indiana
State license required for plumbing and home inspectors. For all other trades, please contact the local government where you intend to contract.

Indiana Professional Licensing Agency
302 West Washington Street, Room E034
Indianapolis, IN 46204-2700
317-234-3022
http://www.IN.gov/pla/

Iowa
Contractors must register with the Iowa Workforce Development department.

Registration includes compliance with workers' compensation law and an unemployment insurance (FUTA) employer account number.

Iowa Workforce Development
1000 East Grand Avenue
Des Moines, IA 50319
800-JOB-IOWA
http://www.iowaworkforce.org/labor/index.html

Kansas

State licensing not required. Please contact the local government where you intend to contract.

Kentucky

State licensing required for plumbing, HVAC. For all other trades please contact the local government where you intend to contract.

Department of Housing, Buildings, and Construction
1047 US Highway 127 South, Suite 1
Frankfort, KY 40601
502-564-3580
http://hbc.ppr.ky.gov/

Louisiana

Commercial and Residential contractors licensure is required. Separate licensure is required for plumbing, and asbestos abatement trades.

Licensing Board for Contractors
P.O. Box 14419
Baton Rouge, LA 70898
225-765-2301
http://www.lslbc.state.la.us/

Maine

State license required for plumbing and electrical trades. Companies selling home repair services must be registered with the state. For all other trades, please contact the local government where you intend to contract.

Department of Environmental Protection
17 State House Station

Augusta, ME 04333
207-287-7688
http://www.state.me.us/dep/index.shtml

Maryland
License required for electrical, plumbing, HVACR, and home improvement. For all other trades, please contact the local government where you intend to contract.

Division of Occupational and Professional Licensing
500 N. Calvert St., 3rd floor
Baltimore, MD 21202
410-230-6270
www.dllr.state.md.us

Massachusetts
State license required for construction supervisors, plumbing, electrical, landscape architecture, and home improvement trades

McCormack State Office Building
One Ashburton Place, Room 1301
Boston, MA 02108
617-727-3200
http://www.state.ma.us/bbrs/hic.htm

Michigan
State license required for residential contractors, plumbing, and electrical. For all other trades, please contact the local government where you intend to contract.

Department of Labor & Economic Growth
P.O. Box 30245
Lansing, MI 48909
517-241-9254
http://www.michigan.gov/cis

Minnesota
Residential contractors need to be licensed. If you work in two or more trades, certain trades will require a license. Call the state for details.

Department of Commerce, Licensing Division
85—7th Place East, Suite 600
St. Paul, MN 55101-3165
651-296-6319
http://www.state.mn.us/cgi-bin/portal/mn/jsp/home.do?agency=Commerce

Mississippi
State license required for commercial jobs over $100,000, city or county jobs over $50,000.

Mississippi Contractors License Board
215 Woodline Drive, Suite B
Jackson, MS 39232
601-354-6161
http://www.msboc.state.ms.us/

Missouri
State licensing not required. Please contact the local government where you intend to contract.

Montana
State license required for plumbing, electrical, and crane operating trades. For all other trades, please contact the local government where you intend to contract.

Department of Labor and Industry
P.O. Box 8011
Helena, MT 59604-8011
406-444-7734
http://erd.dli.state.mt.us/

Nebraska
State license is required for the electrical trade. No state license is required for general contracting, however, local licensure is needed in counties with populations over 100,000. Please contact the local government where you intend to contract.

Nebraska Workforce Development—Department of Labor
5404 Cedar Street
Omaha, NE 68106

402-595-3051
http://www.dol.state.ne.us/

Nevada
Contractors License required for all trades

State of Nevada
Contractors Board—Reno Office
9670 Gateway Drive, Suite 100
Reno, NV 89511
775-688-1141

http://nscb.state.nv.us/

New Hampshire
State licensure required for certain specialty trades. For more information please
contact the local government where you intend to contract.

New Jersey
State licensure is required for plumbing and electrical contractors. For all other
trades, please contact the local government where you intend to contract.

Department of Community Affairs
Bureau of Homeowner Protection
New Home Warranty Program
P.O. Box 805
Trenton, NJ 08625-0805
609-530-8800
http://www.state.nj.us/dca/index.html

New Mexico
Contractors License required for most all trades.

Regulation and Licensing Department
Contractors Licensing Services Inc.
3211 Coors Blvd. SW Suite A-3
Albuquerque, NM 87121
http://www.contractorsnm.com/contact.html

New York
State licensing not required. Please contact the local government where you intend to contract.

North Carolina
A contractor's license is required for all jobs over $30,000. Separate boards license plumbing and electrical trades.

North Carolina Licensing Board for General Contractors
P.O. Box 17187
Raleigh, NC 27619
919-571-4183
www.nclbgc.org

North Dakota
A contractor's license is required for all jobs over $2,000.00. Separate boards license plumbing and electrical trades.

Secretary of State
600 East Boulevard Avenue, Dept. 108
Bismarck, ND 58505
701-328-355665
www.state.nd.us/sec

Ohio
State licensing is required for plumbing, electrical, HVAC, refrigeration and hydronics trades. For all other trades, please contact the local government where you intend to contract.

Ohio Construction Industry Examining Board
P.O. Box 4409
Reynoldsburg, OH 43068
614-644-3493
http://www.com.state.oh.us/ODOC/dic/dicocieb.htm

Oklahoma
Resident electrical, mechanical, and plumbing contractors must be licensed. There are special requirements for non-resident contractors. Please contact Oklahoma Tax Commission for details.

Oklahoma Tax Commission
2501 Lincoln Blvd.
Oklahoma City, OK 73194
405-521-4437
http://www.oktax.state.ok.us/

Oregon
License Required for Commercial and Residential Contractors

Construction Contractors Board
P.O. Box 14140
Salem, OR 97309-5052
503-378-4621
http://www.ccb.state.or.us

Pennsylvania
State licensing not required. Please contact the local government where you intend to contract.

Rhode Island
A contractor's license is required for work on one to four-family dwellings. Licenses are required for electrical, plumbing, and mechanical work.

Department of Administration
Contractor's Registration Board
One Capitol Hill
Providence, RI 02908-5859
401-222-1268
http://www.crb.state.ri.us

South Carolina
A state license is required for commercial work over $5,000.00, and residential work over $200.00. For all other licensing requirements, please contact the local government where you intend to contract

South Carolina Department of Labor, Licensing, and Regulation
Synergy Business Park,
Kingstree Building,
110 Centerview Dr., Suite 306
Columbia, SC 29210

803-896-4696
http://www.llr.state.sc.us/POL/ResidentialBuilders/

South Dakota

No state license is required. A license is required for asbestos, plumbing, electrical, and well drilling trades. For all other licensing requirements, please contact the local government where you intend to contract

Professional and Occupational Licensing
118 West Capitol
Pierre, SD 57501
605-773-3153

Tennessee

Contractors License Required

Licensing Contractors Board
Home Improvement
500 James Robertson Parkway, Suite 100
Nashville, TN 37243-1150
800-544-7693
http://www.state.tn.us/commerce/boards/contractors/index.html

Texas

Licensing required for electricians. Separate boards license HVAC and plumbing. However, contact the Department for most up-to-date information on licensing changes.

Texas Department of Licensing and Regulation
PO Box 13489
Austin, TX 78711
800-803-9202
www.license.state.tx.us

Utah

A contractor's license is required for all trades.

Division of Occupational and Professional Licensing
PO Box 146741
Salt Lake City, UT 84114

801-530-6628
http://www.commerce.utah.gov

Vermont
Licensure is required for asbestos, plumbing, and electrical trades. Certifications required for other trades. For all other licensing requirements, please contact the local government where you intend to contract

Department of Labor & Industry,
National Life Building, Drawer 20
Montpelier, VT 05620
802-828-2288
http://www.state.vt.us/labind/

Virginia
A contractor's license is required for all trades. Separate boards license plumbing, electrical, HVAC, gas fitting, and asbestos trades.

Department of Professional and Occupational Regulation,
Board for Contractors
3600 West Broad Street
Richmond, VA 23230-1066
804-367-8500
http://www.dpor.virginia.gov

Washington
Contractors License Required.

Department of Labor & Industries, Contractors Regulation Section
P.O. Box 44450
Olympia, WA 98504-4450
800-547-8367
https://wws2.wa.gov/lni/bbip/contractor.asp

West Virginia
Contractors License Required

West Virginia Contractor Licensing Board
Building 6, Room B-749
State Capitol Complex

Charleston, WV 25305
304-558-7890
http://www.labor.state.wv.us

Wisconsin

Contractors are required to have the correct credentials for their trade. Not all classifications require credentialing. For a list of credentials, see the website.

Department of Financial Institutions
345 West Washington Avenue
P.O. Box 7846
Madison, WI
608-261-7577
http://www.commerce.state.wi.us/SB/SB-DivProgramsListed.html

Wyoming

State license is required for electrical trades only. For all other licensing requirements, please contact the local government where you intend to contract.

State of Wyoming, Electrical Board
Department of Fire Prevention & Electrical Safety
Cheyenne, WY 82002
307-777-7288
http://wyofire.state.wy.us/

0-595-34551-4

Printed in the United States
26530LVS00004B/115-573